The New Book of Breads

The
New Book
of Breads

Dolores Casella

Illustrated by Janice Lief

David White   Port Washington, New York

This book is dedicated to the memory of my daughter,
Lourice Alexandra.
And to Martha Olson of Sandy, Utah,
my spiritual mother, whose love and devotion
has been a beacon of light through triumph and tragedy.

Library of Congress Cataloging in Publication Data
Casella, Dolores
The New Book of Breads.
Includes Index.
1.   Bread.   I.   Title
TX769.C37   641.8'15   79–22700
ISBN 0–87250–032–2

Manufactured in the United States of America
Drawings by Janice Lief
Design by Kathleen Cushman

Table of Contents

Foreword

My views on baking have not changed a great deal during the years since my first book, *A World of Breads*, was published. I still love to bake bread, and now bake it for another generation of children.

A World of Breads was, I believe, the first book devoted entirely to baking breads to have been published in some 20 years. Since it was published in 1966 there have probably been several dozen books written about the art of bread baking. Why then another one?

Of all the reasons I have for writing this book, the most important is to encourage another generation to approach baking bread with creativity and imagination. And to encourage them to appreciate, and make use of, the flexibility of bread recipes.

With the exception of cake recipes, most of which are rather delicately balanced, I consider all recipes as blueprints subject to improvisation and change rather than as absolute rules. It is an attitude I try to encourage whenever I give demonstrations, talks or lessons. I also like to stress the importance of visual appeal. The time taken to brush a baking loaf with beaten egg white, or to brush the finished loaf with butter, or to braid or twist the loaf before setting it to rise that last time, is always time well spent. Food that looks good tastes good.

Since I entertain a great deal, I am always looking for new ways in which to present food. If I am serving small tea sandwiches, I will bake a huge loaf of crusty bread — either white, rye or pumpernickel, depending on the type of sandwich I'm making — cut off the top, and hollow out the loaf. I use this hollowed loaf as a container for the sandwiches and put the lid on at an angle. I also frequently use hollowed-out smaller loaves of any crusty bread as containers for dips. The loaves, surrounded by crisp, fresh vegetables give a very pleasing effect. And any teenagers in the family will love the dip-soaked bread container the next day.

More than ever before cooking is "in." People are experimenting more, learning more, and enjoying it more. Foods that were once considered "fancy" are now considered everyday items. And certainly the advent of those marvelous appliances, the crock pot and the food processor — especially the food processor — has made certain cooking procedures so simple that we are now able to prepare with ease dishes that once were considered too difficult for the home kitchen.

For the dedicated cook, this is a glorious age.

The Basics of Breadmaking

METHODS

The techniques of bread baking have been changed and added to since I wrote my first book on breads in 1966. The various yeast and flour companies have worked overtime devising methods to make bread-making easier and thus encourage people to make their own breads. Every possible means of combining ingredients has been thought of, and if you don't get confused, some of the methods work very well. The resulting bread isn't quite like that which grandmother made, but then times have changed. And it has been my observation that grandmother wasn't always the good cook she is now cracked up to be. Nostalgia plays a big part in all of our memories, including those about how good the cooking was in the "good old days."

And, of course, the reason that grandma didn't need a cookbook was that her repertory wasn't that big. After all, cooking must have been a bit easier in the days when decisions were made on the basis of what was available, and when available foods were strictly seasonal. I may be a lone voice in the land, but I'm rather glad that I don't live in the days when, if it's Sunday it must be roast beef, and if it's Tuesday it must be hash. I enjoy modern conveniences and modern quick methods.

Can Do Quick Bread

This method of breadmaking, from the Betty Crocker Kitchens, combines yeast and baking powder, and uses buttermilk and the electric mixer to make a quicker bread that is delicious. It is really a development of an old, old method of combining yeast and baking powder. The mixing is new.

2 packages active dry yeast
3/4 cup lukewarm water
1-1/4 cups buttermilk
4-1/2 to 5 cups stirred and
    measured white or
    unbleached white flour
1/4 cup any kind of
    shortening, butter, or
    margarine
2 tablespoons sugar
2 teaspoons baking powder
2 teaspoons salt

Proof yeast in the water in a large electric mixer bowl. Add the buttermilk, 2-1/2 cups of the flour, the shortening, sugar, baking powder, and salt. Beat with an electric mixer on low speed, scraping the sides often, for 2 minutes.

Stir in remaining flour. The dough will be soft and slightly sticky. Remove dough to a lightly floured surface and knead for about 5 minutes. Shape dough into a loaf and place in a greased 9-inch loaf pan. Cover and let rise until doubled in bulk. Brush with melted butter and bake in a preheated 425° F oven, on the lowest rack, for 30 to 35 minutes, or until loaf tests done. Brush with butter again upon removing loaf from the pan.

To Make 2 Loaves: Double all ingredients except for the yeast. Use 3 cakes yeast instead of 4.

CHEESE BREAD. Omit shortening and add 1 cup grated Cheddar cheese with the second addition of flour.

The Coolrise Method

If you are frequently interrupted during the course of a day, yet like to bake your own bread, the "Coolrise" method, out of the Robin Hood Flour Kitchens, might be just your method. Preparing the dough, made by a specially formulated recipe which should *not* be used as the basis for improvisation, takes from 45 minutes to an hour of your time. It then rises in the refrigerator for from 2 to 24 hours. Therefore you can mix up the dough at night for the next night, or to be baked in the morning for the evening meal.

Coolrise Bread

5-1/2 to 6-1/2 cups stirred and measured white or unbleached white flour	2 tablespoons sugar
	1 tablespoon salt
	1/4 cup soft butter or margarine
2 packages active dry yeast	2-1/4 cups hot tap water

Combine 2 cups of the flour, the yeast, sugar, and salt in a large bowl. Stir to blend and then add the soft butter or margarine. Add the hot tap water to the ingredients all at once and beat with the electric mixer on medium speed for 2 minutes, scraping the sides of the bowl occasionally.

Add 1 more cup flour and beat at high speed for 1 minute. Stir in just enough of the remaining flour to make a soft dough that leaves the sides of the bowl. Turn dough onto a lightly floured surface and shape into a ball. Knead until dough is smooth and elastic then cover with a towel and let rest for 20 minutes.

Punch dough down and shape into 2 loaves. Place in greased 8-inch loaf pans, brush tops of dough with oil and cover loosely with waxed paper, brushed with oil, and then with a plastic bag or wrap. Refrigerate for from 2 to 24 hours.

When ready to bake, remove from refrigerator, remove wrappings, and let stand at room temperature for 10 minutes. Bake in a preheated 400° F oven for 35 to 40 minutes, or until loaves test done.

The Easy Mixer Method

Out of the Pillsbury Kitchens came the "Easy Mixer" breads. The electric mixer does most of the work for the busy cook. You use instant skim-milk crystals (something that I have always advocated), which eliminates scalding milk, and you use easy-to-pour vegetable oil instead of shortening. These breads also require less kneading than the conventional breads.

Easy Mixer White Bread

2-1/2 cups lukewarm water	1 tablespoon salt
2 packages active dry yeast	1/3 cup vegetable oil
1/2 cup skim-milk crystals	7 to 7-1/2 cups stirred and
2 tablespoons sugar	measured white or
	unbleached white flour

Pour the water into a large electric mixer bowl. Add the yeast, milk crystals, sugar, salt, oil and 3-1/2 cups of the flour. Beat with the electric mixer on low speed, scraping the sides occasionally. Beat for 3 minutes then on medium speed. Add remaining flour, 1/2 to 1 cup at a time, just until it forms a stiff dough. Cover and let the dough rest for 20 minutes.

Turn dough out onto a lightly floured surface and knead for 1 minute. Divide dough into 2 parts and shape into loaves. Place in greased 9-inch loaf pans, cover and let rise until doubled in bulk. Bake in a preheated 400° F oven for 30 to 35 minutes, or until loaves test done. Makes 2 loaves.

Easy Mixer Cereal Bread

This is my favorite of the newer breads. It's great for sandwiches.

2-1/2 cups lukewarm water	1 tablespoon vegetable oil
2 packages active dry yeast	2 tablespoons bottled brown
2 cups all-bran cereal	gravy coloring
2 cups bite-sized shredded wheat	4-1/2 to 5-1/2 cups stirred and
1 or 2 tablespoons brown sugar	measured white or
1 tablespoon salt	unbleached white flour

Pour water into large electric mixer bowl and add yeast, cereals, sugar, salt, oil, gravy coloring and 2 cups of the flour. Blend and then beat for 3 minutes at medium speed, scraping the sides of the bowl occasionally.

Gradually add enough of the remaining flour to make a stiff dough. Cover the dough and let it rest for 15 to 20 minutes. Turn dough out onto a lightly floured surface and knead for 1 minute.

Divide dough into 2 parts and shape each into a loaf. Place loaves on a greased cookie sheet that has been sprinkled with corn meal, cover and let rise until light. Brush dough with a beaten egg white and bake in a preheated 400° F oven for 25 to 30 minutes, or until loaves test done. Makes 2 loaves.

Quick Yeast Methods

The RapidMix Method, developed by Fleischmann's Yeast Test Kitchens, is probably the most widely known of the newer methods. It uses, as do most of these newer recipes, active dry yeast. The yeast is not proofed in water, but is blended into the other dry ingredients. One of the nice things about this method is that you do not have to stick to the recipes provided by the test kitchens. It is simple to convert your favorite recipe to RapidMix. I am not including a sample recipe here as there are various recipes using the RapidMix method throughout the book.

Red Star Yeast Company developed the *Instant Blend Method* of yeast baking, another method which can be used with any favorite recipe.

How to Convert Any Recipe to Instant Blend

1. Measure the liquid used in the recipe (except eggs) into a pan. Add shortening, sugar and salt. Warm to lukewarm, stirring constantly.

2. Measure into a mixing bowl as many cups of flour as there are total cups of liquid using step 1. Add an additional 1/4 cup flour for each egg called for in recipe. Blend in the yeast.

3. Pour warmed liquid mixture into flour and yeast mixture. Add eggs, if called for. Beat for 1/2 minute at low speed, scraping bowl occasionally.

4. Beat 3 more minutes at high speed. Stop mixer and stir in any fruit, nuts or dark flour called for in the recipe.

5. Gradually add enough white flour to form a soft dough. Then proceed according to recipe directions.

Red Star's Seven Up Refrigerator Dough

5 to 5-1/2 cups stirred and measured white or unbleached white flour	1/4 cup butter or margarine
2 packages active dry yeast	1/4 cup sugar
1 cup 7 Up	1 teaspoon salt
1/2 cup water	1 egg at room temperature
	3 egg yolks at room temperature

Measure 2 cups of the flour into a large electric mixer bowl. Add yeast and blend. Measure 7 Up, water, butter, sugar, and salt into a pan. Heat until warm, stirring. Pour into flour-yeast mixture. Add egg and egg yolks. Beat 1/2 minute at low speed, scraping sides of bowl occasionally. Beat 3 more minutes at high speed. Stop mixer and add more flour, a little at a time, to form a soft dough. Turn onto a lightly floured surface and knead until smooth. For *refrigerated dough,* place in a large, greased bowl, rub surface of dough with oil, cover with waxed paper and then with foil. Refrigerate for 4 hours to no more than 3 days for best flavor and results. Punch dough down every 30 minutes for the first few hours until it is chilled, and then once or twice a day.

When ready to make coffee cake, rolls, or small loaves, remove necessary amount of dough. Shape as desired and place on greased baking sheets or in pans. Cover and let rise until doubled. *This should take no more than 30 to 45 minutes.*

Bake as directed in the following variations.

The dough may be used without prior refrigeration. Simply let it rise until doubled, punch it down, let it rest for 15 minutes, then shape it as desired.

Apricot Cream Cheese Coffee Cake

1/4 portion of 7 Up Refrigerator Dough	3 tablespoons orange or pineapple juice
3/4 cup apricot preserves	1/2 cup sugar
8 ounces cream cheese	1/4 cup sliced almonds

Take 1/4 of the basic dough. Press evenly into a buttered 9-inch layer or square pan. Spread preserves on top of dough. Let rise in a warm place until doubled in bulk, 30 to 60 minutes. While dough is rising, combine cream cheese, orange juice, and sugar for the topping. Just before baking, spread 1/2 cup of the cream cheese topping over preserves. Add almonds. Bake for 25 to 35 minutes in a preheated 375° F oven. Remaining topping will keep in the refrigerator for at least a week, to be used with other coffee cakes, or as a spread.

Pineapple Coconut Coffee Cake

1/4 portion of 7 Up Refrigerator Dough
1/2 cup Streusel (see below)

3/4 cup pineapple preserves
1/2 cup coconut

Take 1/4 of the basic dough and roll out to a 6- by 15-inch rectangle. Spread 1/2 cup of the Streusel over the dough. Roll up from the 15-inch side. Pinch edges to make a roll. Cut, with a very sharp knife, into 15 pieces. Place, cut side up, in buttered 9-inch layer pan. Spread top of dough with preserves and sprinkle with coconut. Let rise in a warm place until doubled in bulk, about 30 to 60 minutes. Bake in a preheated 375° F oven for 25 to 35 minutes, or until done. If coconut is browning too much, place a piece of brown paper over pan.

Remaining Streusel will keep in the refrigerator indefinitely, in a closed container.

STREUSEL. Combine and mix together: 1/2 cup granulated sugar, 2 tablespoons brown sugar, 1/2 teaspoon cinnamon, 1/2 cup finely chopped nuts, 1/2 cup flour, 1/4 cup soft butter, 1 teaspoon vanilla.

If you would like more recipes using any of these methods, simply write to the company which developed the methods. They all distribute recipes, either in booklet or sheet form.

The Sponge Method

Our mothers and grandmothers very often used the sponge method of bread baking. In this method, the liquids, sugar, yeast, salt, and some of the flour are beaten together and allowed to rise as a batter. Then the eggs, remaining flour, and any other ingredients are added, and the dough is allowed to rise for a time before baking.

Some people still prefer this method, and I find that at times it is very convenient. You can convert any recipe to the sponge method.

Use only enough flour to make a thick batter. *If the recipe calls for more than one kind of flour, only use the white flour in the sponge.* When the sponge has risen, simply stir it down and then continue with the recipe according to individual recipe instructions. Many people think that this method produces a bread of finer texture.

Breadmaking is Flexible

The single most important thing to remember about bread baking is that it is far more flexible than other types of cooking or baking. Once you have baked bread for a while, you will become aware of the limits and boundaries within which you have enormous flexibility. You can experiment with different flours and grains, or with other added ingredients such as cheese or cooked sausage. The Italians knead pitted ripe olives (well-drained) into a plain bread dough for a delicious snack bread. *Sausage en Croûte* doesn't have to be baked in a brioche dough. Why not roll the cooked sausage in a rye dough, or the dough for Mustard Bread? The sausage should be warm. If it is cold the dough will not adhere to it and there will be a separation between the sausage and the bread.

Any dough can be shaped pretty much as you desire, if you only *remember that to bake a loaf free form, you need to add a little more flour for a firmer dough that will hold its shape.* Any bread dough can be baked as either rolls or loaf bread. A recipe can be made richer by substituting eggs for part of the liquid — *each large egg will replace 1/4 cup of liquid.* Herbs in any combination that you enjoy can be added to just about any bread dough.

Leftover herb bread makes excellent croutons or bread stuffing. I never throw away stale bread. Stuffing is always best when it's made with a variety of breads, so I have a "stuffing bag" in my freezer, into which I cram all the odds and ends of unused bread pieces. Every now and then I make up a batch of stuffing mix that can be used for baking inside of a bird or for cooking on top of the stove.

Baking should be interesting and fun. Whenever I see a person who has baked without variation the very same bread from the very same recipe for years, I think that she or he is missing out on the *fun* of baking. And don't tell me that that bread is the only kind the family wants or will eat. The fact that they love one kind of bread doesn't mean that they aren't capable of enjoying other kinds also. Experiment — you'll find it rewarding.

The Food Processor

This is the decade of the food processor. This seemingly miraculous machine has brought about a revolution in home cooking, for it accomplishes in seconds what once took minutes. Procedures that were once extremely difficult are now simple. The food processor can quickly make perfect mayonnaise and a fragrant, delicious *aioli* or *taramasalata*, thus allowing the cook to break free of the ubiquitous sour cream dips and sauces. It will chop meat, slice vegetables, and help make almost anything you can imagine, including delicious pastry and a loaf of bread.

Since its capacity is limited, I use the food processor for making only specialty breads, as these are usually made in one-loaf batches. However, the machine works so fast that you can quickly make large batches of bread by simply cutting any recipe into one-loaf batches and making them one at a time.

You can make any bread recipe in the food processor by simply following the instructions given below. Conversely, you can prepare by hand almost any recipe that calls for the food processor.

1. Proof the yeast in lukewarm milk or water. It should be dissolved when added to the processor bowl, *unless the recipe calls for the RapidMix method of combining dry yeast with the flour.*

2. Measure the flour and salt into the processor bowl. If the recipe calls for butter or margarine, don't melt it. Simply cut each bar into 8 pieces and distribute it around the flour in the bowl. Now process the mixture until the butter is cut into the flour. This will take about 20 seconds.

3. Add the yeast mixture, pouring it in through the tube, and process it for just a few seconds. Now add the eggs, if called for, and the remaining liquid ingredients. As soon as the dough is properly mixed it will form a ball and whirl around the bowl.

4. Now remove the ball of dough from the bowl and continue as you would for any bread.

A few bread recipes using the food processor will demonstrate the technique.

Onion Garlic Bread

This recipe and the following Bran Bread recipe are from my friends Rosemary and Bill Slattery of Rhode Island. The recipe makes a small, fragrant loaf of highly flavored bread. Cut it into thin slices and serve it with cheeses and cold cuts.

1 medium onion	1 cup stirred and measured
2 or 3 large cloves garlic	white or unbleached white
1 package active dry yeast	flour
1/2 cup lukewarm water	1 cup stirred and measured rye
1 tablespoon honey or sugar	flour
	1 tablespoon salt

Purée the onion and garlic in the food processor. The purée provides most of the liquid for the bread, resulting in a very strongly flavored onion bread. Proof the yeast in the water with the honey. Add all dry ingredients to the processor bowl and turn the machine on. Slowly add the water-yeast mixture. If no ball of dough forms within a minute, or two at the most, add a tablespoon of water. Keep adding another tablespoon of water every 30 seconds until a ball of dough forms. If the ball has formed and is too wet, add 2 tablespoons of flour every 30 seconds until the dough is the consistency you want.

Remove the ball of dough from the machine, knead it very lightly on a lightly floured surface (the machine will do most of the kneading for you), then place in a clean bowl and rub the surface of the dough with a little oil. Cover and let rise until doubled in bulk. When the dough has risen, punch it down and shape into a loaf. Place in a greased 8-inch loaf pan or simply shape the loaf on a small greased baking sheet. Let the bread rise until doubled in bulk again and bake in a preheated 350° F oven 40 minutes, or until it tests done. Cool on a rack for several hours before slicing. Makes 1 loaf.

Bran Bread

From Rosemary and Bill Slattery, who have "His" and "Hers" food processors.

1 cup bran flakes
3/4 cup lukewarm water
1 package active dry yeast
1 cup stirred and measured
    white or unbleached
    white flour

1/3 cup honey or brown sugar
2 tablespoons molasses
1/3 cup raisins or other
    dried fruit

Combine bran, water and yeast. Set aside to proof the yeast. Turn all other ingredients into the food processor bowl. Turn machine on and add the proofed yeast-bran mixture. The contents of the bowl will form a ball. When this happens, turn the machine off. Remove dough, knead it very lightly on a lightly floured surface and then place it in a clean bowl. Spread with a little oil, cover and let rise until doubled in bulk.

When dough has doubled, punch it down and form it into a loaf. Place in a greased 8- by 3-1/2-inch loaf pan. Cover and let it rise again. Bake in a preheated 350° F oven for 40 minutes, or until bread tests done. Remove to a rack to cool. Cool overnight before cutting, or for at least several hours. Makes 1 loaf.

Brioche

This dough makes perfect rolls, loaf bread, sweet bread, or wrap to be used with Beef Wellington or with *Sausages en Croûte*. The baked loaf is firm enough to make an excellent base for tea sandwiches, especially thin onion sandwiches. The dough holds its shape nicely enough to be used for intricate braids and twists for special occasions. If you wish to use the dough as the basis for a sweet roll, increase the sugar to 1/4 cup. If you glaze the sweet rolls or breads, sprinkle the glaze with sugar.

1 cake yeast
1/3 cup warm milk
1 tablespoon sugar
3 cups stirred and measured
    white or unbleached
    white flour

1-1/2 teaspoons salt
3/4 cup cold or frozen butter,
    cut into at least 8 pieces
3 large eggs, beaten

Proof the yeast in the warm milk with the sugar. Add flour, salt and butter to the food processor bowl. Process until the butter is about the size of corn kernels. Pour in the yeast mixture and process until it is mixed in. Add the eggs and process until the dough forms a ball on the blades.

Turn the dough out onto a lightly floured surface and knead until elastic. This will take just a few minutes as the processor will have accomplished most of it. Place dough in an oiled bowl and turn to oil the dough all over. Cover and let rise until doubled in bulk.

When the dough has doubled, punch it down and knead it a few times. Shape as desired, into any kind of loaf or roll. The baked loaf will be firm and compact. This amount of dough will make an 8- or 9-inch loaf, a tube loaf, or about 2 dozen rolls, depending on the size. The bread or rolls must rise again until doubled and then bake in a preheated 375° F oven for 30 to 35 minutes for the loaf, or 20 to 25 minutes for rolls.

BRIOCHE BRAID. Divide dough into 3 pieces. Roll each into a rope. The ropes should be of equal length. Place ropes side by side. Tuck the ends of the side ropes under the end of the center rope and fold the ends under just so that it doesn't come apart. Braid the ropes and tuck the other end under. Cover and let rise until doubled in bulk. If the braid hasn't risen quite enough it will crack and break during the baking. Brush with Egg Glaze (see below), sprinkle with poppy or sesame seeds, and bake in a preheated 375° F oven for 30 to 35 minutes, or until loaf tests done.

BRIOCHE CHEESE BRAID. Make as above, only knead 1 to 1-1/2 cups of diced cheese into the dough before braiding.

EGG GLAZE. Beat 1 egg yolk with 1 tablespoon milk or water and brush over dough just before placing in oven. You can brush the bread or rolls again during the baking.

Mustard Bread

This makes one of my favorite specialty loaves. I always use it as part of a sausage-cheese tray, along with Onion Garlic Bread and thin, thin slices of a good rye or pumpernickel. The following recipe is adapted somewhat from a recipe in the James Beard book *New Recipes for the Cuisinart.*

2 cakes yeast	2/3 cup stirred and measured rye flour
1/2 cup lukewarm water	
1 teaspoon sugar	1 teaspoon salt
1 cup stirred and measured white or unbleached white flour	1/4 cup butter or margarine cut into 4 pieces
1 cup stirred and measured whole wheat or graham flour	1/2 cup good mustard, preferably a Dijon-type mustard
	1/4 cup lukewarm water

Combine yeast, water, and sugar. Let proof for 5 minutes. Add the flours, salt, and butter to the food processor bowl. Process until the butter is the size of kernels of corn. Add mustard and process until distributed. Add the yeast mixture, processing the entire time, and then slowly add the remaining 1/4 cup water and process until the dough forms a ball. The dough will be heavy and sticky. Rub with oil, place in a clean bowl, cover and let rise until doubled in bulk, 1 to 1-1/2 hours. When dough has doubled, punch it down and let it rise again. Then shape into a loaf and place in a greased 8-inch loaf pan. Cover and let rise until doubled again and then bake in a preheated 375° F oven for 35 to 45 minutes, or until loaf tests done. Cool on a rack before cutting.

Food Processor Hot Rolls

These dainty rolls are so exquisite that I wouldn't want you to miss them. So, if you don't have a processor, just make them the way you would any bread or roll. They are very rich, so I recommend cutting or shaping them into small rolls. *You can use evaporated milk in place of the whipping cream, or half and half, or plain, scalded and cooled milk, or reconstituted skim milk powder, or broth, or water.*

3 cups stirred and measured white or unbleached white flour	1/2 cup butter or margarine cut into 8 pieces
1 teaspoon salt	1 cake yeast dissolved in 1/4 cup lukewarm water
2 large eggs, beaten	
1 cup whipping cream	

Pour the flour and the salt into the food processor bowl. Distribute the butter pieces over the dry mix and process until the pieces of butter are about the size of corn kernels. With machine on add remaining ingredients. Process until the dough forms a ball. Remove ball of dough from machine, rub with oil, cover and let rise until doubled in bulk. *The dough can be refrigerated for up to 24 hours at this point, after which you must allow it to come to room temperature before shaping.*

When dough has doubled, punch it down and shape into rolls as desired. Sometimes I roll the dough out and cut it into rolls with a small biscuit cutter.

Place rolls on a greased cookie sheet, cover and let rise until doubled. Preheat oven and bake at 375° F until browned and done, about 20 minutes. Makes about 24 rolls.

SWEET ROLLS. For a sweet roll you can add 2 tablespoons sugar to dough along with 1 teaspoon of grated orange rind. Bake as directed and then frost with powdered sugar thinned with orange juice and flavored with more grated rind.

Beaten Biscuits

The American South's most famous contribution to the roster of homemade bread has been updated. These small biscuits used to require 30 to 45 minutes of beating with a rolling pin or club before they were properly blistered and ready to bake. The use of the food processor eliminates that. I use these biscuits, split, as the base for all kinds of spreads.

3 cups stirred and measured white or unbleached white flour	3/4 cup lard, butter, or margarine
2 teaspoons salt	3/4 cup ice water or icy cold milk

Measure flour and salt into processor bowl. Turn machine on and off quickly to combine ingredients. Cut butter or lard into 8 to 10 pieces and distribute over flour mixture. Process until mixture is the size of corn kernels. With machine running, pour liquid into mixture in a steady stream. Process until mixture forms a ball and then continue processing for another 2 minutes. *This eliminates the need for beating the dough.*

Remove dough from bowl to a lightly floured surface. Roll dough out to a thickness of approximately 1/8 inch. Now fold the sheet of dough over onto itself. This makes 2 layers of dough. Cut into rounds with a biscuit cutter. Place on an ungreased baking sheet and bake in a preheated 350° F oven for 25 minutes, or until golden brown and done. Remove from oven and serve immediately. If you wish to use these as the base for spreads, split the biscuits while hot and return them to the oven for an additional 2 or 3 minutes. Makes 48 biscuits.

Crock Pot Breads

When my children were younger I had three crock pots: a small 2-quart one in which I would cook cereals overnight so that they would be ready when the children got up; a slightly larger one for cooking vegetables; and a 5-quart one for general, all-around crock pot cookery. They made life much easier on those busy, busy days when I was lucky to keep track of which way I was going. The crock pot is here to stay, and while its best use is for the long, slow cooking of various stews and braised dishes, it can also be used for a few breads.

Not all breads can be cooked in a crock pot. However, some breads can, and of course any bread, pudding, or cake that requires steaming is ideal for the crock pot.

Baking Frozen Bread Loaves in the Crock Pot

Generously grease a loaf pan that will fit the bread. Place frozen dough in the pan and place in a crock pot. Cover and heat on low for 2 to 3 hours, or until bread is thawed and beginning to rise. Turn temperature control to high and continue baking for another 2 to 3 hours, or until bread is browned and done.

Heating Bread or Rolls in the Crock Pot

The crock pot is excellent for heating rolls, doughnuts, muffins, and hot dog or hamburger buns. Simply place in crock pot, cover and heat on low for 30 to 45 minutes. If baked goods are frozen, increase temperature control to #2 and heat for an hour to an hour and 15 minutes, or until baked goods are thawed and hot.

Baking Bread in the Crock Pot

Some authorities say that bread should be baked in a pan right on the floor of the crock pot. Others pour 2 cups of hot water into the crock pot surrounding the pan containing the quick or yeast bread dough. I don't think that it makes much difference, with the obvious exception of those breads which require steaming, in which case the water would be necessary. I've included two recipes, one by each method. Any quick bread recipe can be baked just as the Banana Bread recipe instructs. I don't think that the crock pot works as well for yeast breads. However, I know many people do use it for these breads. Baking instructions are simple. Bake on high for 2 to 3 hours. Test carefully before removing the bread

Boston Brown Bread

Whenever I serve Boston baked beans I make some Boston Brown Bread in the crock pot. This is excellent. You will need two 1-pound coffee cans.

1 cup stirred and measured white or unbleached white flour, or rye flour	1 cup corn meal
	1 teaspoon salt
	1-1/2 teaspoons baking soda
1 cup stirred and measured whole wheat or graham flour	2/3 cup molasses
	2 cups sour milk or buttermilk
1 cup raisins	

Combine and stir together the dry ingredients. Combine liquid ingredients and stir into the dry ingredients, stirring just enough to moisten all ingredients. Stir in the raisins. Turn mixture into 2 well-greased 1-pound coffee cans. Cover tops with foil and tie. Place cans on a rack in the crock pot and pour 2 cups very hot water around the cans. Cover crock pot and cook on high for 2-1/2 to 3 hours. Remove cans and cool on a rack for 5 to 10 minutes before turning out. Slice and serve hot with butter. Makes 2 loaves.

Crock Pot Banana Bread

This makes an absolutely yummy banana bread. The recipe will also make 2 dozen muffins, made in regular sized, greased muffin tins and baked in a preheated 350° F oven for 20 to 25 minutes, or until muffins test done.

3/4 cup butter or margarine
1-1/2 cups sugar
3 large eggs, beaten
1/2 cup mashed banana
1/4 teaspoon vanilla extract
1/4 teaspoon banana flavoring,
　optional

2 cups stirred and measured
　white or unbleached white
　flour
1 teaspoon baking powder
1/2 teaspoon baking soda
1/2 teaspoon salt

Cream together the butter and sugar. Add the eggs, mashed banana and flavorings and mix well. Combine dry ingredients and stir together. Add to liquid mixture and mix lightly, just until dry ingredients are thoroughly moistened. Do not overmix. Turn batter into a well-greased 9-inch loaf pan. Place pan in crock pot and set on high. Bake for 2 hours. Do not remove cover during this time. At the end of 2 hours, test the bread in several spots with a toothpick or cake tester. It should come out clean. If not, continue baking for 15 minutes. Test again. If it still isn't done, continue baking, testing at 15-minute intervals. Cool loaf on a rack and let sit overnight before cutting. Makes 1 loaf.

The Freezer

I would hate to have to live without a freezer. For years I yearned for one, considering it a luxury. Now I consider the one I own as indispensable as the food processor. Besides making it possible for me to take full advantage of food sales, my freezer enables me to save valuable time. I never make just one *moussaka*, or one meatloaf, or soup for one meal only. It is just as easy to make a huge pot of spaghetti sauce or beef stew as a small one. The extra always goes in the freezer to save time for another day.

　I love to entertain and I like to look unruffled and cool with my guests. The freezer makes this possible, for I can prepare many items ahead so that the last minute work is kept to a minimum. And of course I always have bread of all kinds in the freezer.

　Any bread can be frozen once it is baked and cooled. However, freezing unbaked dough is usually rather chancy for the yeast occasionally loses its leavening power, and the loaves are sometimes tough. The following recipe, though, is one that was evidently developed specifically for freezer use, and the lady who gave me the recipe says that she has never had a bit of trouble with it. I have tried it a number of times myself, always successfully. Follow instructions carefully.

White or Whole Wheat Freezer Bread

This very good bread can be made with part whole wheat flour if desired, in which case I would recommend using brown sugar in place of the white.

12 to 13 cups stirred and measured white or unbleached white flour, or a mixture of white and whole wheat flour	3 tablespoons salt
	4 packages active dry yeast
	1/3 cup soft butter, margarine, or lard
1/2 cup granulated or brown sugar	1 cup instant skim milk powder dissolved in 4 cups warm water or potato water
	1 cup wheat germ

This recipe is made by the RapidMix method of combining the yeast with the dry ingredients. In a large mixer bowl combine 4 cups of the flour with the sugar, salt, and yeast. Stir to blend. Then add the butter and reconstituted milk. Beat for 3 minutes with an electric mixer, scraping the sides of the bowl occasionally. Add 1 more cup flour and beat at high speed for 2 minutes. At this point you will probably have to remove the dough to a larger bowl. Then add the wheat germ and enough of the remaining flour to make a firm dough.

Turn dough out onto a lightly floured surface and knead until smooth and elastic, about 8 to 10 minutes. Cover the dough with a towel and let it rise, right on the lightly floured surface, for 10 to 15 minutes. The dough will loosen up and be easier to work with.

Shape the dough into 3 or 4 loaves and place on a greased baking sheet. Cover and freeze until solid. Remove loaves from sheet and bag. Seal and return to freezer. *These are best when used within a month.*

When ready to use, remove loaves to be used from freezer. Remove wrappings. Cover and let stand at room temperature until thawed, from 3 to 4 hours. Then shape the dough as desired and place in greased 8- or 9-inch loaf pans. Cover and let rise until doubled in bulk and then bake in a 350° F oven for approximately 45 minutes, or until browned and done. Makes 3 or 4 loaves.

BASIC BREAD INGREDIENTS

Yeast

It is the yeast that you use that leavens the bread, that makes it rise until light, and that gives it that marvelous yeasty odor while baking. The kinds of yeast are interchangeable. *One cake of compressed yeast equals one package of active dry yeast equals one tablespoon active dry yeast bought in bulk.* I use the active dry yeast exclusively because it is simpler to use. I wouldn't dream of buying it in those little expensive 1/4-ounce packages. I buy it in a 2-pound container and occasionally order a 5-pound package from the local health food store. It is less than one half the cost of the 1/4-ounce packages. And if you bake often you have the assurance that it is always there.

Compressed yeast will keep for a week or two under refrigeration. The active dry yeast will keep indefinitely when frozen, and can be removed and used when you wish. It will also keep for a year under refrigeration.

One cake of yeast will raise up to 8 cups of flour. This is the "rule" that the old-time cooks used when making bread, and that's why they set their pan of dough to rise overnight. Naturally it takes longer for a cake of yeast to raise 8 cups of flour than it takes for 2 cakes of yeast to raise the same amount. The amount of yeast used can be varied by the cook according to her or his needs. *The maximum amount of yeast to use is 1 cake of yeast to each cup of liquid, or 1 cake of yeast to each 3 cups of flour.* However, for some people, this amount of yeast results in *too* yeasty a bread. If you want to increase the amount of yeast, I recommend doing it gradually to see if your family likes the yeastier flavor. If you bake a lot, I recommend using the active dry yeast, buying it in quantity, and keeping it in an airtight container in the refrigerator.

Liquids

As you can see by a quick glance through the recipes in this book, there is a broad range of liquids that can be used in breads. The most commonly used are milk, water, and potato or macaroni water. However, you can also use beer, chicken or beef broth or even wine. Wine is usually blended with another liquid such as milk. *Wine makes the milk curdle, but this has no effect on the finished loaf.*

Water provides a crisper crust and a more honest flavor. Most of the great breads of the world are made with water, and I frequently substitute water for whatever other liquid is called for, depending of course on what kind of bread it is, and what flavor I want. Milk produces a browner crust and the bread will keep longer. Potato or macaroni water results in a coarser loaf and a slightly larger one. The other liquids are for flavor, although each has an effect on the finished loaf.

In place of regular milk you can use diluted evaporated milk, evaporated skim milk, half and half, or skim milk powder. *The skim milk powder, which is very fine, can be stirred into the flour. The skim milk crystals should be reconstituted by adding to water.* As an equivalent to 1 quart of milk use 1/2 to 2/3 cup skim milk powder, or 1-1/2 cups skim milk crystals. When I was baking bread for my children to grow on, I always doubled the amount of skim milk powder necessary to make the amount of milk called for. In other words, if the recipe called for 2 cups of milk, I used 2 cups of water and enough skim milk powder to make the equivalent of 4 cups. This resulted in an important increase in protein and calcium for children who, like my tiny grandsons, would live on bread and peanut butter if allowed.

Flour

A hardwheat, unbleached flour still makes the best bread dough. Lacking that, use the regular unbleached all-purpose flour that is available throughout the country now. But buy a *good* flour. The quality of the loaf of bread that you produce depends on the quality of the ingredients that go into it. That basic rule applies to any phase of cooking or baking. *You simply cannot produce a superior product with inferior ingredients.*

I don't sift flour and never have, although in previous books I have recommended sifting the flour for bread baking. At that time I believed that beginning cooks should always sift. Now I think that they should do what is comfortable for them.

I have a friend who purchases wheat by the 100-pound sack and she supplies me with all of the freshly ground whole wheat flour that I use. I buy all other whole grain flours and corn meal at the health food store. The difference in flavor between a good whole grain flour and the dead kind that is sold from supermarket shelves is enormous.

If you do a lot of whole grain baking, buy the flours that you use most often in large quantities and store them under refrigeration or in the freezer. I have always found two refrigerators a necessity. The smaller one I use to store grains, extra produce, or other perishable items.

You will, if you bake much at all, occasionally be puzzled by a recipe requiring more or less flour at different times. I have a favorite Oatmeal Bread recipe (it is in *A World of Breads*) that in Los Angeles took 10 or 11 cups of flour, and here, in Idaho Falls where it is much higher and drier, only requires 8 cups of flour. Don't be put off by the discrepancy. Different brands of flour, or the same brand at different times or in different areas of the country, will absorb varying amounts of liquid. The usual proportion is 1 cup of liquid to 3 or 4 cups of flour. However, in any bread recipe I recommend using the first half of the dry ingredients and then stirring in the remaining flour, *1 cup at a time,* only until enough flour is used to make a medium or a firm dough. That method eliminates any problem.

Sugar

Sugar aids in browning the crust, but most of the time I think it is unnecessary, and can be either eliminated or at least reduced without hurting the bread. I use sugar in sweet breads and coffeecake and desserts, but in other recipes I either eliminate it or cut its amount considerably. We eat too much sugar, and its harmful effects on the body are well known. I was told once of a salad dressing that was said to be out of this world. I tracked down the recipe and discovered that it called for 3/4 cup of sugar in a recipe that made one quart of dressing! I was appalled. I never made it, and I hope I never taste it.

Where sugar is called for in the bread recipes, you can use interchangeably either granulated sugar, light or dark brown sugar, or raw sugar.

Shortening

At one time I abhorred lard, and didn't use it at all. I've since changed my mind, and I now think that the best shortening for almost any kind of bread is a combination of butter and lard. For small yeast rolls that I serve on special occasions I do often use all butter. However, margarine, shortening, bacon fat, butter, or lard can be used interchangeably in most breads. The latter three will each give its own distinctive flavor to the bread.

Salt

Salt gives flavor and stabilizes the fermentation. The usual proportion is 1 teaspoon salt to each 2 or 3 cups flour. You can reduce the salt or omit it completely from any bread recipe.

Eggs

Eggs are added for richness and flavor. They are especially used in European coffee breads. Substitute 2 yolks for each whole egg called for, and the bread will be richer yet.

HOW TO'S

Kneading

Unless otherwise specified, bread dough requires kneading. However, I have rarely found it necessary to knead the 10 to 15 minutes usually specified. Some very heavy or very rich doughs require a long kneading time, but most bread doughs will do very nicely on 5 to 8 minutes of kneading time.

The dough should always be turned out onto a lightly floured surface and kneaded with the hands, turning the dough and folding it over on itself, until smooth and elastic. If more flour is needed for the surface, use as little as possible, as too much flour kneaded into the dough will make a tough loaf of bread.

Rising

The kneaded dough should be placed in an oiled bowl and turned so that the surface of the dough is oiled all over. This prevents a crust from forming. The dough must be covered with a clean towel, a piece of waxed paper or a tent of foil.

The length of time for rising always depends on how much yeast has been used, and how warm your kitchen is. Bread dough will rise much more quickly on warm summer days than during the winter.

When it has risen enough it will look rounded and full. Press one or two fingers into the dough. If the dough holes fill up quickly, the dough has not risen enough. If the impressions made by your fingers remain, the dough is ready for the next step. If you cannot continue with the recipe at that time, simply punch the dough down and let it rise again. *Each time it rises, it will rise more quickly.*

Shaping The Dough

One of the reasons I wrote my first book, *A World of Breads,* was that I was annoyed with the unnecessarily complicated and time-consuming methods recommended by most cookbooks. I still see new books that recommend rolling bread dough out into a rectangle, and either rolling the dough up like a jelly roll or folding it like an envelope to achieve the loaf shape. How silly!

Simply divide the dough into the number of loaves it will make. A dough using 3 cups of flour will usually make a loaf that fits an 8-inch loaf pan. A dough using 4 cups of flour will make a loaf that fits a 9-inch loaf pan. However, remember that bread dough is flexible. If I don't have an 8-inch loaf pan, I simply end with a slightly smaller, flatter loaf by using a 9-inch loaf pan. If out of 9-inch loaf pans, you can make an 8-inch loaf and some rolls. When baking bread simply use your imagination and remain flexible.

When the dough is divided into the number of loaves you wish, knead each piece of dough to press out any air pockets, and then use your hands to shape the dough. How simple. You can use the standard loaf pans, or, if you have made a slightly firmer dough, you can shape either long or round loaves to bake on greased baking sheets. Or you can use the Bake-a-Round glass cylinder to make a perfectly round loaf of bread. The Bake-a-Round is made of oven-proof glass and fits into a special holder for baking and handling. It's fun to use, and a recipe using 3 to 4 cups of flour fits it perfectly. Follow instructions that come with the Bake-a-Round.

If you bake bread often, it's fun to try some different shapes. Even bread baked in a loaf pan can be braided before it is placed in the pan, twisted by making 2 ropes and twisting them together. The better food looks the better it tastes, and I always like to increase its visual appeal.

Greasing The Pans

Always use margarine or shortening of some kind to grease pans. *Don't use oil.* The dough seems to absorb the oil and invariably sticks.

Baking

All of the breads in this book were made in an electric oven, and the oven was checked before beginning. If your bread doesn't bake in the time recommended, or if it overbakes, either have your oven checked, or make allowances for its vagaries.

Homemade Mixes

TIME-SAVING convenience foods, without the additives and preservatives that we are continually warned against, *are* available. Not on the grocer's shelves, but in your own home, made in minutes and stored for instant use. The homemade mixes can be made as nutritious as you desire by the use of whole grains, wheat germ and soy flour. They will *always* be more flavorful than the commercial products. And a very important added benefit is that when you make them yourself you have far more variety available than any grocer can carry. For *any* bread that you enjoy can be made into a mix.

For example, suppose you especially enjoy Whole Wheat French Bread. You can't make up extra loaves on baking day, because you don't have a freezer. But you *can* make it into a mix, thereby cutting your preparation time rather substantially. Simply take the *dry* ingredients and multiply them by however many loaves you want to have mix for. Say you want a mix that will make 5 loaves. Stir and measure 5 cups unsifted gluten flour, 10 cups whole wheat or graham flour and 10 cups white flour. Add the 5 tablespoons of salt and 5 to 10 packages of active dry yeast. Mix these ingredients thoroughly in a plastic storage container or a heavy-duty plastic bag. Store them, preferably in the refrigerator. When you are ready to bake, shake the mix vigorously and measure out 5 cups of mix for each loaf of bread. Stir in 2 cups of warm water and the required olive or vegetable oil, and proceed as directed in the recipe. If you wish, you can omit the yeast from the stored mix, and add it when ready to bake, proofing it first in the liquid ingredient.

If you don't have a freezer, this does save a certain amount of time. As I mention so often throughout the book, it pays to experiment. If an experiment fails, all you've lost is a few ingredients, and a little time. If it succeeds, you've gained immeasurably.

Success Tips for Homemade Mixes

1. If you wish, you can substitute a whole wheat pastry flour for regular whole wheat or graham flour.

2. Please remember that different flours absorb liquids at different rates. If a recipe seems too dry, add a little more liquid, a tablespoon or so at a time, until the mixture is right.

3. By the same token, if a recipe is too moist, add a little more flour, a tablespoon at a time, until the mixture is right.

4. It is not necessary to sift the flour. Simply stir it well, so that it is *loose,* and then spoon it lightly into a cup measure and level off the top. Do *not* shake the cup to settle it.

5. When you use wheat germ, wheat germ flour, or soy flour in a mix, the mix should be stored in the refrigerator or freezer. In fact, it is best to store *any* mix using *any* whole grain flour in the refrigerator or freezer. If you buy flours in a health food store they will contain no preservatives. This makes them much more healthful and *much* more flavorful, but does limit their shelf life. They will keep in the refrigerator for months, though, and when kept in the freezer they will stay good for years.

USING THE MICROWAVE OVEN. The microwave is perfect for any muffin which has ingredients which will supply color — whole wheat or whole grain muffins, for example. Do not use metal pans. Use instead a double thickness of paper muffin cups. Fill the cups just 1/2 full instead of the traditional 3/4 or 2/3 full, because the muffins will rise more than usual in the microwave. Set the oven for #8, or high, and bake 2 muffins for 45 to 60 seconds. If you are baking 4 muffins allow 45 seconds to 1-1/2 minutes, and for 6 muffins allow 1-

1/2 to 2 minutes. If you are using the Six-Week Muffin Mix, or *any* chilled batter, allow another 12 to 15 seconds baking time.

Homemade Biscuit Mix

This only takes minutes to prepare and is far better than the commercial mix. It can be enriched with the addition of a little wheat germ and/or soy flour if desired. Please read Success Tips before beginning.

Basic Mix

| 8 cups white or unbleached white flour, stirred and measured | 1/4 cup baking powder
4 teaspoons salt
2 cups lard or shortening |

Combine ingredients in a 4- or 5-quart mixing bowl. Cut the lard in until the mixture resembles a very coarse corn meal. Store in a 5-quart plastic storage container, or in a heavy-duty plastic bag. If made with lard, or if you use wheat germ or soy flour, the mix must be kept in the refrigerator or freezer. Otherwise it can be kept in a cool, dry storage area.

Biscuits

To make biscuits, shake the Basic Mix until it is thoroughly mixed. Measure 3 cups of the mix into a bowl. Add 1/2 cup milk or thin yogurt and 1 large egg to the mix all at once. Stir together for 20 to 25 strokes. If it is too dry add some more milk, no more than a tablespoon at a time. Turn mixture out onto a lightly floured bread board and knead *very* lightly, only until it just holds together. Pat the dough out to a thickness of 1/2 inch or a little more, and cut with a floured glass or cookie cutter. Bake on a greased cookie sheet in a preheated 450° F oven for 10 to 12 minutes, or until browned and done. Makes about 2 dozen biscuits.

Cornbread

To make cornbread, shake the Basic Mix until it is thoroughly blended. Measure 1 cup into a mixing bowl. Add and stir in thoroughly: 1-1/2 teaspoons baking powder and 1 cup yellow cornmeal. Now break 2 or 3 large eggs into a measuring cup and add milk to bring it to 1-1/4 cups. Stir this together and pour into the dry ingredients. Mix thoroughly. Pour into a greased, preheated 9-inch square baking pan. If you want an especially crisp cornbread (to go with soup, for example) use a 9- by 13- by 2-inch baking pan. Bake in a preheated 400° F oven for 20 to 30 minutes.

Banana-Nut Bread

To make banana-nut bread, shake the Basic Mix until it is well mixed. Measure 2 cups mix into a bowl. Cut in 1/4 cup butter or shortening until the size of small peas. Mix together: 2 large eggs, 1 cup sugar (preferably a mixture of brown and white), 1 cup mashed soft bananas, 1 teaspoon vanilla extract. Stir this into the mixture along with 1/2 to 3/4 cup chopped walnuts or pecans. Stir carefully, just so that the ingredients are well moistened. As with muffins, you do not want to overmix! Pour into a greased 9- by 5- by 3-inch loaf pan. Let stand for 15 minutes, then place in a preheated 350° F oven and bake for 1 hour, or until a toothpick stuck in the center comes out clean. Place the pan on a rack and cool for 5 minutes, then turn the bread out of the pan and continue cooling on the rack. This freezes especially well. If you wish to slice it very thin, wrap the thoroughly cooled bread and store in the refrigerator for 24 hours before slicing.

Six-Week Muffin Mix

This is a wet mix, not a dry mix. It is simple, has superb flavor, and makes tender, hot muffins. Just stash it away in the depths of your refrigerator, and bring it out at strategic moments. You can even disguise it with various additions, adding them just before baking. Remember that even a "quickie" dinner takes on added interest when served with a fresh, hot bread of any kind. Please read Success Tips before beginning.

Basic Mix

4 cups bran flakes
2 cups granola
2 cups boiling water
1 cup soft shortening,
  margarine, or butter
2 to 3 cups sugar, part brown
  and part white

4 large eggs, beaten
1 quart buttermilk
5 cups white or unbleached
  white flour, stirred and
  measured
5 teaspoons baking soda
2 teaspoons salt

Pour the boiling water over the bran flakes and granola. Add the shortening. Add the sugar, eggs and buttermilk. Combine the flour, baking soda, and salt and stir to mix well. Add to the bran mixture. *Do not overmix.* The ingredients should be thoroughly moistened but that's it. This will yield approximately 6 quarts.

Store in airtight plastic storage containers in the refrigerator. Bake at your convenience, using as little or as much batter as needed. Any additions to the batter should be added at baking time. Fill greased muffin tins no more than 2/3 or 3/4 full and bake in a preheated 400° F oven for 20 to 25 minutes, depending on the size of the muffins.

VARIATIONS. You can use 6 cups of bran flakes and omit the granola. *Or,* you can use 2 cups *each* of rolled oats, bran flakes, and crumbled shredded wheat biscuits. Everything else remains the same. Any of the variations are excellent.

When ready to bake add 1/2 to 1 cup of any of the following: grated, drained, fresh apple; blueberries; well-drained, crushed pineapple; chopped dried figs, apricots, dates, raisins, or prunes; chopped raisins and sunflower seeds. Or add 1/4 cup grated orange rind or a few caraway seeds with some grated lemon rind.

Whole Grain Rolled Oat Mix

A very adaptable mix, especially favored by children for the delicious cookies it produces. Please read Success Tips before beginning.

Basic Mix

6 cups whole wheat or graham flour, stirred and measured	3 cups old-fashioned rolled oats
2 cups rye flour, stirred and measured	4 teaspoons salt
	3 tablespoons baking powder
	1 tablespoon brown sugar

2 cups skim milk powder
(non-instant type)

Combine ingredients in a 4 or 5-quart plastic storage container, or in a heavy duty plastic bag. Shake vigorously to thoroughly blend the ingredients. Store in a cool, dry spot, preferably in the refrigerator.

VARIATIONS. You can omit the rye flour and use all whole wheat flour if desired. For a lighter product you can substitute a few cups of white flour for the same amount of whole wheat flour.

Biscuits

To make biscuits, shake the Basic Mix vigorously so that it is thoroughly blended. Measure 2-1/2 cups of mix into a bowl. Stir in 1/2 cup water, milk or thin yogurt mixed with 1 large egg. Stir together until it forms a ball in the bowl. This may be rolled and cut as for regular biscuits, or you can make drop biscuits. Bake on a greased baking sheet in a preheated 425° F oven for 10 to 12 minutes, or until browned and done. It depends on the size of the biscuits.

Muffins

To make muffins, shake the Basic Mix vigorously so that it is thoroughly blended. Measure 2-1/2 cups mix into a bowl. Combine 3 tablespoons vegetable oil, 1 cup water, milk or thin yogurt, 1 large egg and 1 or 2 tablespoons honey. Mix together and stir into the dry mix. Stir just until moistened. *Do not overmix.* Spoon into greased muffin tins, filling no more than 3/4 or 2/3 full. Bake in a preheated 400° F oven for 20 to 25 minutes, or until browned and done. Makes 12 to 14 muffins.

Pancakes

To make pancakes, shake the Basic Mix vigorously so that it is thoroughly blended. Measure 2 cups of mix into a bowl. Add 1 cup buckwheat flour, 1/4 cup vegetable oil, 1 large egg, 2-1/2 cups water, milk or thin yogurt, and 2 tablespoons honey. Stir until well mixed. Bake as usual on a lightly greased griddle.

Cookies

These are too good to leave out. Shake the Basic Mix thoroughly. Measure 3 cups mix into a bowl, add 3/4 cup rolled oats, 1/2 cup raisins or chopped dates, and 1/2 cup chopped walnuts or pecans. Stir together. Now add 3/4 cup honey and 1/2 cup vegetable oil and 1 large egg. Stir together until well mixed and lumpy, but thoroughly moistened. Drop by the teaspoonful onto greased cookie sheets. Allow room for spreading. Bake in preheated 350° F oven for 10 to 15 minutes, or until done.

Whole Wheat Bread Mix

Use this mix to make a hearty dinner bread, or add the fruit and nuts to yield a healthful sweet bread. Read Success Tips before beginning.

Basic Mix

14-1/2 cups whole wheat or graham flour	3 tablespoons baking soda
8 cups white or unbleached white flour, stirred and measured	1 cup brown sugar 1/2 cup white sugar

Combine ingredients in a 9-quart plastic storage container, or in a heavy duty plastic bag. Seal, or fasten securely, and shake vigorously to mix. Store in a cool, dry spot until needed.

Wheat Bread

4 cups whole wheat bread mix	1 cup milk
1/2 cup (1 stick) butter or	2 tablespoons lemon juice or
margarine	vinegar
1 large egg	

Shake the Basic Mix until it is thoroughly blended. Then measure 4 cups of the mix into a bowl. Using a pastry blender or your fingers, cut the butter in as you would for pastry. Combine the milk and lemon juice and let it set until it is soured, about 10 minutes. Now make a well in the center of the dry ingredients. Pour the soured milk and the egg into the well. Stir together until you have a fairly stiff dough. If the dough is too stiff and dry, add a little more milk (it does not have to be soured). Add it very, very slowly, a tablespoon at a time, mixing the ingredients until of the proper consistency. If the dough is too moist, add white flour the same way.

Turn the dough out onto a very lightly floured bread board and knead it for 7 or 8 minutes. It should be smooth. Form the dough into a rounded loaf. It might help to wet your hands just a little to facilitate this. Place the loaf on a greased cookie sheet and bake it in a preheated 400° F oven for 45 to 50 minutes, or until crusty and browned. Cool the loaf on a rack.

FRUIT BREAD. For each loaf of bread add 1/3 cup of raisins or dates, 1/3 cup chopped walnuts or pecans, and/or 2 tablespoons chopped candied fruits. Continue as directed.

Whole Wheat - Wheat Germ Quick Bread Mix

This is my personal favorite among the quick bread mixes. It not only tastes delicious, but is so full of good things that you will feel absolutely virtuous when you prepare dishes with it. Experiment, since it can certainly be used for many more dishes than I have the space to include. Be sure to read Success Tips before beginning.

Basic Mix

6 cups whole wheat or graham flour, stirred and measured

3 cups white or unbleached white flour, stirred and measured

3 cups soy flour, stirred and measured

2-1/2 tablespoons salt

1/2 cup baking powder

1-1/2 cups skim milk powder (non-instant kind)

3-1/2 cups wheat germ

Combine ingredients in a 6-quart plastic storage container, or in a heavy-duty plastic bag. Seal, fasten securely, and shake vigorously to mix. Store in a cool, dry spot, preferably the refrigerator or freezer.

Pancakes

To make pancakes, shake the Basic Mix until it is thoroughly mixed. Measure 1-1/2 cups into a bowl. Add 1 large egg, 1 cup milk or thin yogurt, and 2 tablespoons vegetable oil. Stir until smooth. Bake on a hot griddle. You can use any of your favorite pancake variations with this recipe. This makes about 10 pancakes.

Biscuits

To make biscuits, shake the Basic Mix until it is thoroughly blended, and measure 4 cups into a mixing bowl. Stir 2/3 cup vegetable oil, 1 large egg, and 1 cup milk or thin yogurt into the mix. Stir together just until the ingredients are all moistened. Turn onto a lightly floured bread board and knead very lightly, just enough to make the ingredients hold together. Pat the dough out to a thickness of 1 inch and cut with a floured glass or biscuit cutter. Place close together on a greased cookie sheet. Preheat oven and bake at 425° F for 12 to 15 minutes, depending on the size of the biscuits.

VARIATION. To make cobblers or drop biscuits, simply add another egg and a little more milk to make a dough that will drop from a spoon.

Muffins

To make muffins, shake the Basic Mix until it is thoroughly blended. Measure 2-1/2 cups into a mixing bowl. Combine 2 large eggs, 1 cup milk or thin yogurt, 2 tablespoons vegetable oil and 3 tablespoons honey and beat together. Pour this into the mix and stir together just until blended and moist. *Do not overmix.* Spoon into greased muffin tins filling them no more than 2/3 or 3/4 full. Bake in a preheated 400° F oven for 15 minutes. You can use any of your favorite muffin variations with this recipe. Makes 12 to 14 muffins.

Nut Loaf

To make a good nut loaf, shake the Basic Mix until it is thoroughly blended and measure out 3 cups into a bowl. Add 1 to 1-1/2 cups chopped nuts and mix together. Combine 2 large eggs, 3/4 cup milk or thin yogurt, 2/3 cup brown or white sugar, and 1/2 cup vegetable oil and mix together. Stir this into the dry mix and stir together until thoroughly blended and moistened throughout. Turn into a well-greased smaller loaf pan, about 8- by 4- by 2-1/2-inches. Bake in a preheated 350° F oven for 50 to 60 minutes, or until the loaf tests done. You can use any of your favorite quick nut bread variations with this recipe.

Cornell Formula Homemade Mix

The use of wheat germ and soy flour makes this excellent mix especially nutritious. The corn meal adds a bit of crunch, and the whole thing is rich and full of flavor. Again I recommend experimenting with the mix. You will probably come up with more variations than I have listed. Please read Success Tips before beginning.

Basic Mix

7-1/2 cups whole wheat or
    graham flour (you can use
    part white flour)
3/4 cup soy flour
1-1/2 cups bran flakes

1-1/2 cups wheat germ
1-1/2 cups yellow corn meal
1-1/2 cups skim milk powder
    (non-instant kind)
2 tablespoons salt

1/3 cup baking powder

Combine ingredients in a 6-quart plastic storage container, or in a heavy duty plastic bag. Seal, fasten securely, and shake vigorously to mix. This mix should be stored in the refrigerator or freezer.

VARIATIONS. You can add to the mix any or all of the following: 1/3 cup sesame or sunflower seeds; 1 cup chopped dates, raisins, walnuts, or pecans. If you don't like soy flour, replace it with regular flour. A cup of the flour can be replaced with buckwheat or rye flour, or with rice polish.

Pancakes

To make pancakes, shake the Basic Mix until it is thoroughly blended. Measure 2 cups of the mix into a mixing bowl. Add 2 tablespoons honey, 1/4 cup vegetable oil, 3/4 cup milk or thin yogurt, and 2 large eggs. Mix until moistened. If the mix is still too dry, add another egg or a little more milk. Bake as usual for pancakes. If you have any batter left over it will keep in the refrigerator, covered, overnight. In the morning simply stir it to remix. The batter will be a little thinner. Makes 12 good-sized pancakes.

Muffins

To make muffins, shake the Basic Mix until it is thoroughly mixed. Measure 3 cups of the mix into a bowl. Add 3 tablespoons honey or brown sugar, 3/4 cup milk or thin yogurt, 2 large eggs and 1/4 cup vegetable oil. Mix just until the ingredients are thoroughly moistened. Do not overmix. Spoon into greased muffin tins filling no more than 3/4 full. Bake in a preheated 425° F oven for approximately 15 minutes. You can use any usual muffin variation with this mix, adding the ingredients when you mix up the batter for baking. Blueberries are especially nice.

Note. The muffin recipe can be used to make delicious dumplings. Just mix as directed and drop into stew or soup.

Biscuits

To make biscuits, shake the Basic Mix until it is thoroughly mixed. Measure 4-1/2 cups of the mix into a bowl. Add 2/3 cup vegetable oil, 1 cup milk or thin yogurt, and 2 large eggs to the mix. Stir together just until the mix is thoroughly moistened. Turn onto a lightly floured bread board and knead very lightly, just enough to make the ingredients hold together. Pat the dough out to a thickness of about 1 inch and cut with a floured glass or biscuit cutter. Place close together on a greased cookie sheet. Bake in a preheated 425° F or 450° F oven for 12 to 15 minutes, or until browned and done.

Quick Sweet Bread Mix

This mix is very simple to put together, and will keep for months in a cool, dry place. The breads made from it take only minutes, and are especially easy because oil is used for the shortening. Please read Success Tips before beginning.

Basic Mix

3 cups brown sugar
2 cups granulated white sugar
5 cups white or unbleached
   white flour, stirred and
   measured
4 cups whole wheat or graham
   flour, stirred

3/4 cup wheat germ (if you do
   not have this, substitute
   whole wheat or graham
   flour)
1 tablespoon baking soda
1 tablespoon double-acting
   baking powder
1 tablespoon salt
1 pound walnuts, chopped (optional)

Combine all ingredients in a large bowl and mix thoroughly. Store in containers in a cool, dry place. The mix can be frozen.

Apple Butter Raisin Bread

2 large eggs
3/4 cup apple butter
1/2 cup corn or vegetable oil
1/2 cup raisins

1 teaspoon cinnamon
1/4 teaspoon each: cloves
   and nutmeg
3 cups Quick Sweet Bread Mix

Combine liquid ingredients and whip until light and well blended. Add raisins and dry ingredients and fold together so that the mixture is thoroughly moistened. *Do not beat.* Pour into a greased 9-inch loaf pan and bake in a preheated 350° F oven for 30 to 40 minutes, or until bread tests done. Cool on a rack, turning the bread out of the pan after

5 minutes. Cool completely before cutting. This bread can be wrapped and frozen.

Banana Bread

Use 2 large eggs, 1 cup mashed soft bananas, 1/2 cup corn or other vegetable oil, 1/2 teaspoon cinnamon, 1 teaspoon vanilla, and 3 cups Quick Sweet Bread Mix. Follow the directions for Apple Butter Raisin Bread, above.

Blueberry Bread

Use 2 large eggs, 1/2 cup corn or other vegetable oil, 1 teaspoon vanilla, 1 teaspoon grated lemon or orange rind, 1 cup frozen, *unthawed* blueberries, and 3 cups Quick Sweet Bread Mix.

Date Bread

Pour 1/2 cup boiling water or orange juice over 1 cup chopped dates. Let cool. Use 2 large eggs, 1/2 cup corn or other vegetable oil, 1 or 2 teaspoons vanilla, 1 teaspoon grated orange rind (if you use the orange juice), and 3 cups Quick Sweet Bread Mix. Follow the directions for Apple Butter Raisin Bread, adding the drained dates with the dry ingredients.

Corn Meal Muffin Mix

This makes a marvelously tasty and nutritious muffin. If your family loves muffins this mix can save you a lot of time and elicit raves.

Basic Mix

2 cups yellow corn meal	1/2 cup brown or white sugar
2 cups whole wheat or graham flour	2 teaspoons salt
1/2 cup wheat germ	2 teaspoons double-acting baking powder
2 teaspoons baking soda	

Combine ingredients in a 1-1/2- to 2-quart plastic storage container, or in a heavy duty plastic bag. Seal, fasten securely, and shake vigorously to mix. Store in a cool, dry spot, preferably the refrigerator or freezer.

Muffins

To make muffins, shake the Basic Mix until it is thoroughly blended, and measure out 1-1/4 cups into a mixing bowl. Now stir together 1 large egg, 1/2 cup yogurt (or sour cream or buttermilk), 2 table-spoons milk and 1 tablespoon vegetable oil. Pour this into the mix and stir together just until blended and thoroughly moistened. *Do not overmix.* Spoon into greased muffin tins. They should be no more than 3/4 full. Bake in a preheated 425° F oven for 15 to 18 minutes, or until browned and done. Makes 1 dozen muffins. You can use any of your favorite muffin variations with this recipe. Blueberries are especially good.

Homemade Self-Rising Flour

In some areas of the country they use a great deal of self-rising flour. In other areas, where it isn't commonly used, it is difficult to find. But it is simple to make. This formula should be used within 30 days for best results. It is worth making if you use a lot of self-rising flour.

5 pounds stirred and measured white or unbleached white flour	1/2 cup baking powder 1/4 cup baking soda 1/4 cup salt

Stir together thoroughly and store in a large plastic storage container. Shake thoroughly before using.

If you only use self-rising flour occasionally, use the following formula: For every cup of self-rising flour called for, substitute 1 cup stirred and measured white or unbleached white flour mixed with 1-1/4 teaspoons baking powder and a pinch of salt.

Homemade Baking Powder

Many cooks do not like to use commercial baking powders. It's true that the chemicals and additives do sometimes add a slightly bitter aftertaste. Homemade baking powder is very simple to make. The two main ingredients are baking soda—either potassium bicarbonate, which one buys at a drug store, or sodium bicarbonate, which is in every grocery store—and cream of tartar. Make your baking powder in small quantities, because the fresher it is the more effective it will be.

2 parts cream of tartar	1 part baking soda or potassium
2 parts cornstarch or arrowroot	bicarbonate (see above)

Combine the above ingredients thoroughly. Store in an airtight container so that it doesn't lump, and use in the same proportions as any commercial baking powder.

White Breads

BREAD is basic, perhaps the most basic of all prepared foods. Most of us respond to the smell of fresh baked bread, even when we might not respond to some other food fragrance. Even those who were not brought up on homemade bread react enthusiastically to its smell. I have been baking all of my bread for more years now than I care to remember, and I still enjoy it and look forward to its baking.

There *is* a mystique about bread baking. It defies the perfect "rule." You must still use intuition to decide how much flour to add, and when the dough has risen or baked long enough. You must always consider factors influencing the recipe. For example, in Idaho Falls, where it is higher and drier than on the coast where I lived when I wrote my first two books, it takes less flour to make a proper dough.

Some people, though, still insist on trying to bring the bread baking to the laboratory and set absolute rules for it. I read recently of one man who had bread baking down to a science. He weighed and measured everything so that the finished loaf was "perfect," whatever "perfect" means.

I made that bread and it neither tasted nor smelled any better than the loaf that I bake most often (Quick Loaf Bread, on page 45), which is certainly the simplest bread I have yet come across. The "perfect loaf" did not appeal to my tiny grandsons any more than the simple bread I fry on the griddle for them to eat hot, cut open, and slathered with butter. It did not appeal to the company that I tested it on any more than my usual homemade bread does, and it certainly didn't appeal any more to me.

Or perhaps I just resented the idea that someone could end the mystique of bread baking by taking it on a thorough trip through the laboratory.

Success Tips for White Breads

Flour. White flour and unbleached white flour are virtually the same thing. Although the unbleached is better for you the two are interchangeable. If you can find unbleached *bread* flour, which is a hard, winter wheat flour, this is always the best for any kind of bread. This flour is usually available in health food stores or from local millers.

The amount of flour given in bread recipes is always approximate, since different flours vary in their ability to absorb moisture. Moisture absorbence also depends on climate and elevation. The important thing is to add just the amount of flour needed to make the kind of dough — soft, medium, or firm — that the recipe calls for. Flour does not need to be sifted. Just stir it, spoon it into a measuring cup and level off the top.

Sweetening. Honey and granulated sugar can be used interchangeably in yeast breads. The use of honey changes the liquid balance of the recipe, but since you are using an approximate amount of flour instead of an exact amount as you would in a cake, the difference doesn't matter. In fact, you can substitute brown sugar or a combination of sugar and molasses, but then you do not have a white bread. Also, the flavor of molasses does not go as well in a white bread as it does in a whole-grain bread.

Yeast. The recipes call for 1 packet, or cake, of yeast. You can use either dry or cake yeast. I always use dry yeast for its convenience, using 1 tablespoon for each cake called for. Unless I am making a RapidMix recipe, where the yeast is mixed in with the dry ingredients, I prefer to proof the yeast in a small amount of water before combining it with the rest of the ingredients. I think that the yeast is incorporated into the dough better that way, and if you are not certain of your yeast, it is a good way to tell if it is still good.

Milk. I find it much easier to use skim milk powder, or the reconstituted skim milk crystals — which are more readily available — in many of the recipes which call for milk. The powder can be stirred in with the flour, and the crystals are easily reconstituted just by stirring them into the water. Neither requires scalding, and you can increase the nutritional value by simply using the amount of liquid called for, but increasing the milk powder or crystals. This is discussed more fully in Success Tips For Whole Wheat Breads (p.125).

Other Liquid Ingredients. You can always use plain water in place of milk. It will change the flavor and keeping qualities, but many people prefer to use water. Your bread isn't going to *fail* if you use water instead of milk, it will just be different. You can also use a mild broth such as chicken broth when it is appropriate — for example in a dinner roll.

Kneading. Instructions for kneading are given in Success Tips For Whole Wheat Breads (p. 126).

Rising. All yeast breads must be allowed at least one rising. Most, but not all, breads require a second rising, and some a third. However, if you are called away and cannot bake a particular bread when it should be, just punch it down and let rise a third, or even a fourth time. It won't hurt. Remember that the bread will rise faster each time. If necessary, any bread dough can stand an overnight stay in the refrigerator. However, not any bread can be used as a refrigerator bread and left there for days on end. Refrigerator breads require more yeast and sweetening to keep them from becoming sour.

Shaping. I cut my dough into as many pieces as I want loaves, and then after kneading out all of the air, I just pat them into shape. Sometimes I make a braid, or a twist. With a tender dough the loaf pan holds them in shape. With a firm dough — and *any bread that is to be baked on a cookie sheet must be made with a firmer dough than* *those breads that are baked in loaf pans* — I sometimes like to make elaborate braids and top them with a twist. This kind of bread must rise exactly until it is double, otherwise the braids will break open during the baking. Any bread dough can be made into loaves, or rolls, or shaped as desired.

Pans. Pan size is the standard 9-inch loaf pan, unless indicated otherwise. Pans and sheets must be brushed with melted or softened margarine, butter, or lard *rather than with oil.* Oil is absorbed by the dough and the loaves will stick to the pan.

Freezing. All breads freeze well *after they are baked.* Simply make certain that they are completely cooled and wrapped carefully. Freezing is recommended for no longer than three months. Thaw at room temperature, or remove from bag, wrap in foil, and thaw in a 325° F oven for 20 to 30 minutes. Thawing in a microwave sometimes toughens the bread. As mentioned elsewhere, for small families I recommend slicing the bread first and freezing in each package only what you will use in a day or two. This way you can enjoy homemade bread without the fear of wasting any.

Nutritional Note. When I make bread for enjoyment only I do not concern myself much with the nutritional value. However, when I was making bread for a growing family, and now when I make it for my grandchildren, nutrition is important. I still recommend the Cornell Formula, developed at Cornell University School of Nutrition. Experiments there proved that the addition of small amounts of soy flour and the other ingredients yielded a bread that was able to sustain life healthily.

Cornell Triple-Rich Formula

1 tablespoon soy flour	1 tablespoon skim milk powder
	1 teaspoon wheat germ

Add the above ingredients to the bottom of each cup of flour before adding the flour. This is done so that the ingredients are not accidentally added to the flour measurement. If you use a particular recipe frequently, make a notation at the side of the recipe as to how many tablespoons of the above ingredients you use. Then make the necessary flour adjustment.

TO USE THE MICROWAVE OVEN. White breads stay white when baked in the microwave, and don't look appetizing. The only way that you can achieve the golden brown crust that we all prefer is to bake them in the microwave and brown them in the regular oven. I would just as soon bake them completely in the regular oven instead of having to bother with changing ovens.

Plain White Bread

This is a simple, basic bread, the kind your mother and grandmother probably made, using lard instead of butter or margarine. I'm giving the recipe as it is traditionally made. However, *I always substitute a cup of skim milk crystals reconstituted with 2 cups lukewarm water instead of the milk that the recipe calls for.* Please read Success Tips before beginning.

2 cups milk	1 cake yeast
2 tablespoons honey or sugar	1/4 cup lukewarm water
2 teaspoons salt	5-1/2 to 6-1/2 cups stirred and
2 tablespoons butter or margarine	measured white or
	unbleached white flour

Heat milk until bubbles form around the edges. Remove from heat and pour into a mixing bowl over the honey, salt, and butter. Cool to lukewarm.

Dissolve yeast in water and let proof for 5 minutes. Pour into cooled milk mixture. Stir in 3 cups of the flour and beat hard until it forms a smooth batter. Then add remaining flour, 1 cup at a time, until it has formed a medium-stiff dough. Turn this dough out onto a lightly floured bread board and knead until smooth and elastic, about 8 to 10 minutes. Place in a lightly greased bowl and turn the dough so that there is a thin film of grease all over. Cover and let rise until doubled in bulk, about 1-1/2 hours.

When dough has risen, punch it down and allow it to rise again. It will take less time the second time. Punch it down again, transfer to a lightly floured surface and cut into 2 parts. Shape each part into a loaf, or into rolls if desired. Place in greased bread pans, cover and let rise until doubled in bulk again. Bake in a preheated 400° F oven for 35 to 40 minutes for loaves, and 20 to 25 minutes for rolls, or until browned and done. Brush with butter upon removing from the oven. Makes 2 loaves or 36 rolls.

Quick Loaf Bread

Although this bread appeared in my first book *A World of Breads*, it is simply too good, too simple, and too useful not to repeat. My youngest daughter started baking at the age of nine, with this bread. It's great for beginners because it is virtually failproof. For extra nutrition you might use 1 cup each of rice polish and wheat germ in place of 2 cups of the flour. You can make an herb bread by adding 3/4 teaspoon each savory and marjoram, 1/4 teaspoon sage and 1/4 cup minced parsley to the dough. For a delicious whole-grain bread you might use 1/2 cup wheat germ and 3-1/2 cups of a good muffin mix (see Homemade Mixes) in place of 4 cups of flour. Please read Success Tips before beginning. And remember that the ease and quick rising of the bread — it takes only 2 hours from start to finish — depend upon the use of the maximum amount of yeast.

4 cups lukewarm water	10 to 12 cups stirred and
4 cakes yeast	measured white or
1 tablespoon to 1/3 cup sugar or	unbleached white flour
honey	2 tablespoons salt

Combine the water, yeast, and sugar or honey. Let proof for 5 to 8 minutes. Then beat in 5 cups of flour and the salt. Beat hard with a spoon until the batter is smooth and bubbly. Now add remaining flour 1 cup at a time, until you have a medium dough. You may have to mix in the last few cups of flour with your hands.

At this point you can knead the dough very lightly — just a few times — with your hands, or else turn it out onto an oiled or very lightly floured bread board, and knead just a few times. Turn the dough into a clean, oiled bowl and turn it so that the surface of the dough is oiled all over. Cover with a towel and let rise until doubled, approximately 30 minutes.

When the dough has risen, punch it down and turn it out onto a very lightly floured board and shape as desired. This amount will make 3 loaves, or 36 rolls, or 3 filled loaves. The plain loaves and the rolls will need to rise until doubled, approximately 20 to 30 minutes. Then bake in a preheated 400° F oven for 30 minutes for the loaves and 20 to 30 minutes for the rolls. For anything else follow the instructions included with the individual variations.

CRUSTY ROLLS. Use a little less flour than called for to make a tender, barely soft dough. Cut the raised dough in half, and then cut each half into 18 pieces. Roll each piece into a roll and twist the roll around your finger to make a twist. Place in buttered muffin tins and let rise until doubled. Bake in a preheated 400° F oven for 30 to 35 minutes, or until golden brown and done. The longer baking time results in a roll that is crusty on the outside and soft and tender on the inside.

BROWN AND SERVE ROLLS #2. Let rise until not quite doubled. Bake in a preheated 275° F oven for 40 minutes, or until done in the middle, but not browned. Remove from oven and cool in the tins for 20 minutes. Then remove from tins and finish cooling. Wrap and store in freezer for up to 2 months, or in the refrigerator for up to 2 weeks. To serve, take directly from refrigerator or freezer and bake in a preheated 400° F oven until browned, approximately 8 to 10 minutes.

FILLED CHEESE BREAD. For this delicious bread, take 1/3 of the dough and roll it out on a greased cookie sheet. The dough should be about 1/4 to 1/3 inch thick. Spread the center strip of dough, lengthwise, with a thin coating of mayonnaise. Sprinkle with minced green onions, or with drained, sautéed white onions. Over this, overlap slices of Cheddar, Jack or Provolone cheese. Any good melting cheese will do, or use a mixture of cheeses if you are stuck with some odds and ends. Sprinkle with a little crumbled oregano and a drizzle of olive oil. Now, fold the ends of the dough over just to cover the ends of the filling. Pull the sides of the dough up and over the filling, overlapping the dough on top and sealing. Carefully flip the loaf over so that the seam side is on the bottom. Slash the top in several places so that the steam can escape. Bake immediately in a preheated 400° F oven until browned and done, about 30 to 35 minutes. If desired the dough can be brushed with beaten egg before baking.

Note. This filled loaf is subject to any number of variations. Once I was out of onions, so I used half a small can of chopped olives. It was delicious. Occasionally I use some crumbled, cooked Italian sausage along with the cheese and other ingredients.

ITALIAN FILLED BREAD. The true name for this bread is one I can neither pronounce properly nor spell. First, saute a minced onion in a small smount of olive oil, just until transparent. Then stir in some minced garlic. Add 5 or 6 nice, fresh tomatoes that have been peeled and seeded and then diced, and 2 tablespoons half and half. Stir together and simmer gently for 30 to 45 minutes, or until the sauce is thick. Add salt and pepper to taste, and some sweet basil and a touch of oregano. While the sauce is cooking, take a pound of fresh Italian sausage, either hot or mild according to your taste, and fry until cooked through. Remove from heat and cut into even slices. To finish the bread you will also need 1/3 to 1/2 cup fresh ricotta or drained cottage cheese, and 1/3 cup grated Romano or Parmesan cheese.

When the dough has risen the first time, and you are all set with cooked sausage and thick sauce, proceed with the dough as directed for the Filled Cheese Bread. Down the center of the dough spread your thick sauce. The sauce should be thick enough so that it does not run. Place the sausage slices over the sauce. Dot with the ricotta and sprinkle with Romano. Drizzle with a little olive oil. Fold the ends over, and then the sides and flip it over so that the seams are on the bottom. Slash the top in several places so that the steam can escape. Let this bread rise for 15 minutes and then bake in a preheated 400° F oven for 30 to 35 minutes, or until browned and done. Remove to a board, and let set for 5 to 10 minutes before slicing. Serve with soup or salad for a light, filling meal.

Note. Of course, to all of that good stuff already in the filling, you can add some nice melting cheese like Jack or Mozzarella.

WEST COAST CHEESE BREAD. This bread is popular on the West Coast. Take enough dough for 1 loaf of bread and roll it out. Spread with 1 cup grated Jack cheese. Roll up as for a jelly roll and place in a well-greased bread pan. Make a deep slit down the center of the loaf and sprinkle it liberally with more grated cheese. Let rise until almost double and bake in a preheated 400° F oven until browned and done, about 40 minutes.

SESAME SEED ROLLS. You will need 1 or 2 cups of sesame seeds for these. Make your rolls, brush them all over with beaten egg and then roll in sesame seeds. Place in greased muffin tins, let rise and bake as usual. Sesame seed bread can be made the same way.

FILLED ROLLS. To make these I take some grated cheese such as Jack or Cheddar and combine it with minced ripe olives and minced green onions. The mixture should hold together well so that you can shape it into medium sized balls and wrap the dough around. Place, seam side down, in greased muffin tins, let rise and bake as usual. These are a pleasant surprise to bite into, and are best served hot.

Favorite White Bread

This slightly sweet bread makes excellent toast. The amount of honey can be cut to 1/3 cup if desired. Please read Success Tips before beginning.

2 cakes yeast	1/3 cup vegetable oil
1/2 cup lukewarm water	2 tablespoons salt
2/3 cup mild-flavored honey	2 large eggs
3 cups hot water	12 cups stirred and measured
1 cup evaporated milk	white or unbleached white flour

Dissolve the yeast in the lukewarm water and proof for 5 to 8 minutes. In a large bowl combine the honey, hot water, canned evaporated milk, oil, and salt. Beat in the eggs. Add the yeast mixture and 6 cups of the flour. Beat together thoroughly. Then add remaining flour, 1 cup at a time, until you have a medium dough.

Turn dough out onto a lightly floured surface and knead lightly. Turn dough into an oiled bowl and rub the surface of the dough with a little oil. Cover and let rise until doubled in bulk, about 1 to 1-1/2 hours. Punch down and let rise for another 45 minutes to an hour.

When dough has risen, punch it down, turn it out onto a lightly floured surface and cut into 3 or 4 pieces. Shape into loaves and place in greased 9-inch loaf pans. Cover and let rise until doubled in bulk again. Bake in a preheated 350° F oven for 45 minutes or until loaves test done. Makes 3 or 4 loaves.

Yogurt Granola Bread

Yogurt can be used in any recipe that calls for sour cream. And granola adds its bit to make this a delicious bread, especially good when toasted and spread with honey butter. Please read Success Tips before beginning.

1-1/2 cups lukewarm water	2 to 3 teaspoons salt
2 tablespoons honey or brown sugar	4 to 5 cups stirred and measured white or unbleached white flour
2 cakes yeast	
2 tablespoons vegetable oil	2 cups any type of granola,
1 cup plain yogurt	preferably with fruit and nuts in it

Combine water, honey, and yeast. Set aside to proof for 5 to 8 minutes. When yeast is ready, stir in the oil, yogurt, salt and 2 cups of the flour. Stir until thoroughly blended. Then add remaining flour, 1 cup at a time, until it has formed a medium-soft dough. Rub the ball of dough all over with some oil, cover and let it rise until doubled in bulk.

When dough has doubled, punch it down and turn it out onto a very lightly floured surface. Knead lightly and then divide into 2 parts. Shape each into a loaf and place in a greased 8-inch loaf pan. Cover and let rise again until doubled and then bake in a preheated 375° F oven for 35 to 40 minutes, or until browned and done. Turn out onto racks to cool.

Note. If you want, you can shape the bread into 2 round loaves and bake on a greased cookie sheet. You can brush the loaf with beaten egg and sprinkle with sugar just before baking, if desired.

Swiss Cheese Bread

An Idaho neighbor gave me a loaf of this delicious bread along with the recipe. I occasionally add several cloves of crushed garlic along with the cheese. This recipe uses the RapidMix method of combining the dry yeast with the dry ingredients.

Please read Success Tips before beginning.

5 cups stirred and measured white or unbleached white flour	2 packages dry yeast
	1 cup each: water and milk
	3 tablespoons butter, margarine,
2 tablespoons sugar	or vegetable oil
1-1/2 teaspoons salt	1-1/2 cups grated Swiss cheese
1 large egg, beaten	

In the large bowl of an electric mixer combine 2 cups of the flour, the sugar, salt and yeast. Heat the water, milk and butter until mixture is lukewarm. The butter does not have to be completely melted. Add the liquid to the yeast mixture gradually, beating with the electric mixer. Beat for 2 minutes.

Add the cheese, egg, and another 1/2 cup of flour. Beat for another 2 minutes. Then stir in the remaining flour to make a soft, sticky dough. Do not try to knead the dough. Simply cover the bowl and let the dough rise until doubled in bulk.

When the dough has doubled, beat it down with a wooden spoon and divide between 2 greased loaf pans, or 2 greased 1-quart casseroles. Cover and let rise until no more than doubled in bulk. Bake in a preheated 375° F oven for 40 to 50 minutes, or until loaves test done. If the loaves brown too soon in the oven, cover with foil. Makes 2 loaves.

Note. The addition of another 1 to 1-1/2 cups of stirred and measured flour, and some kneading, will produce a dough firm enough to be braided and baked on a greased cookie sheet. This makes 1 large braided loaf. Baking temperature and time is the same.

Coffee Can Cheese Bread

This recipe uses the RapidMix method of combining the dry yeast with the flour. It can be baked in a regular loaf pan, but I think it is fun to bake it in a 1-pound coffee can for the nice, round slices. The bread makes delicious toast. Please read Success Tips before beginning.

3 cups stirred and measured white or unbleached white flour	1/2 cup vegetable oil
	2 tablespoons sugar
	1 teaspoon salt
1 package active dry yeast	2 large eggs, beaten
1/2 cup skim milk crystals reconstituted in 1 cup water	1 cup shredded Cheddar cheese

Combine 1-1/2 cups of the flour and the yeast. Combine reconstituted milk with oil, sugar, and salt and heat just until warm. Add the warm liquid mixture to the flour-yeast mixture and beat with an electric mixer about 2 minutes, scraping down the sides occasionally. Beat in the eggs and cheese and then add enough of the remaining flour, plus a little extra if needed, to make a stiff batter. Beat for another minute.

Divide the dough into 2 well-greased 1-pound coffee cans, cover and let rise until light and bubbly, about 1 hour. The dough should be just below the rim of the cans. Bake in a preheated 375° F oven for 35 to 40 minutes or until done. Makes 2 loaves. Loaves should cool in the cans, on a rack, for 10 to 15 minutes before turning out.

Garlicky Potato Bread

This bread has plenty of flavor! It's great with barbecues. Please read Success Tips before beginning.

1 large potato, peeled and diced	1/2 cup dry skim milk powder
1 teaspoon salt	(not the crystals)
1 cup water	3 large eggs
1/2 cup butter, margarine, or	2 cakes yeast
vegetable oil	1/4 cup lukewarm water
3 tablespoons sugar	3 or 4 fat cloves of garlic, crushed

5 to 6 cups stirred and measured
white or unbleached white flour

Cook the potato, salt and 1 cup water in a small saucepan until potato is tender. Remove from heat and add butter and sugar. Beat with electric mixer until mixture is smooth.

Then beat in the skim milk powder and the eggs, beating until mixture is smooth and well blended.

Meanwhile dissolve the yeast in the 1/4 cup water. Add to potato mixture with the garlic. Add 3 cups of the flour and stir until it forms a smooth batter. Add remaining flour, 1 cup at a time, until it forms a medium dough.

Turn dough out onto a lightly floured bread board and knead until smooth and elastic. Turn into a greased bowl, turning the dough so that it is greased on all sides. Cover and let rise until dough is doubled, approximately 1 hour. At this point the dough can be punched down and refrigerated overnight. After this step you must allow the dough to rise at room temperature before shaping into loaves.

Whether or not the dough is refrigerated, it must rise a second time. After the second rising punch the dough down and shape it into 2 loaves or into 16 rolls. Place loaves in greased bread pans, rolls on greased cookie sheets. Cover and let rise until doubled in bulk before baking. Bake in a preheated 375° F oven for 50 to 60 minutes for the loaves or 25 to 35 minutes for the rolls. Remove to racks to cool and brush with melted butter or with cool water.

Bacon And Onion Bread

This makes a nicely flavored bread, good with soup. Please read Success Tips before beginning.

Filling

3 large onions, minced	1/2 teaspoon black pepper
3/4 pound bacon, diced	1 teaspoon paprika

Dough

3-1/2 cups warm water	8 cups stirred and measured white or unbleached white flour
1 cup non-fat milk crystals	
2 tablespoons sugar	2 large eggs, beaten
1/4 cup butter, lard, or margarine, melted	1 teaspoon salt
	2 or 3 tablespoons strong black coffee
2 cakes yeast	

First make the filling. Fry the bacon until crisp. Remove to paper towels to drain. Sauté the onion in the bacon fat until soft and transparent. Remove to toweling to drain. Combine onion, bacon, pepper and paprika.

In a large bowl combine the water, milk crystals, sugar, melted butter, and yeast. Proof for 5 minutes. Then stir in 4 cups of the flour and beat well. Add the eggs and salt and beat to combine thoroughly. Now add remaining flour, 1 cup at a time, just until you have added enough flour to make a soft dough. Turn dough out onto a lightly floured surface and knead until smooth and elastic. Place dough in a large, oiled bowl and turn so that the surface of the dough is spread with a thin film of oil. Cover and let rise until doubled in bulk, about 1 hour.

Turn out onto a lightly floured surface again and divide dough into 2 parts. Roll each part out into an inch-thick rectangle. Spread each with filling and roll up tightly as you would a jelly roll. Place in greased 9-inch bread pans. Cover and let rise again until doubled in bulk.

When ready to bake, use a very sharp knife and make several slashes in the tops of the loaves. Brush all over with the cold coffee and bake in a preheated 375° F oven for 35 to 45 minutes, or until done. Makes 2 loaves.

Italian Pepper Bread

This crackling and pepper-spiced bread is an Italian delicacy that too few people are familiar with. It is especially good when served with a good mustard and assorted cheeses and sausages. Please read Success Tips before beginning.

3/4 to 1 pound salt pork, finely diced	1/4 cup drippings from the salt pork
1-1/2 cups warm water or scalded, cooled milk	2 cakes yeast
1 tablespoon salt	3/4 cup lukewarm water
1 tablespoon coarsely cracked black pepper	6-1/2 to 7 cups stirred and measured white or unbleached white flour

Fry the salt pork until it is crisp. Drain off the fat reserving 1/4 cup to use in the bread. Drain cracklings on paper towels.

Combine warm water with salt, pepper, and drippings. Dissolve the yeast in the 3/4 cup water, letting it stand until the yeast foams. Combine with pepper mixture.

Stir in 3 cups of the flour and the cracklings, beating until it forms a smooth batter. Add remaining flour, 1 cup at a time, until you have a medium dough.

Turn the dough out onto a lightly floured bread board and knead until the dough is elastic. Place in a greased bowl, turning the dough so that it is greased all over. Cover and let rise until doubled in bulk, approximately 1 hour.

When the dough has risen, punch it down, turn it out onto a lightly floured bread board and divide into 2 parts. At this point the dough can be shaped as desired: Divide each part into 3 parts and roll the parts into long ropes which can then be braided together; or the ropes can simply be twisted together; or shape the dough into ovals or rounds on a cookie sheet; or bake in greased bread pans.

However you shape the loaves, they should be covered and allowed to rise again until doubled. Then, just before baking, brush each loaf with a tablespoon of fat and bake in a preheated 375° F oven for 30 to 35 minutes, or until loaves sound hollow when tapped on the bottom with your fingers. Cool on racks. Makes 2 loaves.

Crunchy Italian Loaves

You will love this crunchy bread as much as we do. If you do not have the baquette pans, simply shape the dough into 2 long loaves and bake on a greased, corn meal-sprinkled baking sheet. Please read Success Tips before beginning.

2 cakes yeast dissolved in 2 cups lukewarm water	1 tablespoon honey or molasses
2 tablespoons vegetable oil	2 cups cracked wheat soaked in water to cover and then
1 tablespoon salt	squeezed dry
3-3/4 cups stirred and measured white or unbleached white flour	corn meal

Turn dissolved yeast, oil, salt and 2 cups of the flour into the large bowl of an electric mixer. Beat on low speed for 30 seconds, scraping the sides of the bowl occasionally. Then add the honey and beat for 3 minutes at high speed. Stir in the cracked wheat and then enough of the remaining flour to form a stiff dough. Rub the surface of the dough with oil and cover and let rise until doubled in bulk.

When dough has doubled in bulk, punch it down and turn out onto a lightly floured surface. Knead lightly and then divide dough into 2 parts. Cover and let rise again. Then punch the dough down and shape into long rolls. Turn into 2 greased and corn meal-sprinkled baquette pans. Cover and let rise about 45 minutes. Then cut sharp diagonal cuts into the surface of the dough. Brush with beaten egg white and bake in a preheated 375° F oven for approximately 45 minutes, or until browned and done. For a crisper crust, brush loaves with egg white several times during the baking and then immediately upon removing from the oven. Makes 2 loaves.

Yeast Beer Bread

Any beer can be used in this bread, although the darker the beer the better. This bread is especially good with ham and cheese either in sandwiches or just as snacks. Please read Success Tips before beginning.

1 cup dark beer	1 teaspoon salt
1 cake yeast	1 large egg, beaten
2 tablespoons sugar	1/4 cup butter, margarine, or
3 to 3-1/2 cups stirred and	vegetable oil
measured white or	1/2 cup wheat germ
unbleached white flour	

Warm the beer until it is lukewarm. Pour it into a large mixing bowl and add the yeast. Let set until the yeast foams. Now add the sugar, 2 cups of the flour, the salt, egg and butter. Beat until it forms a smooth batter. Then add the wheat germ and the remaining flour 1/2 cup at a time, mixing until it forms a medium dough. Turn dough out onto lightly floured surface and knead until it is smooth and elastic. Cover, right where it is, and let the dough rise until it is doubled in bulk.

When dough has doubled in bulk, punch it down and shape it into a loaf. Place in greased loaf pan, cover and let rise again until doubled. Bake in a preheated 375° F oven for 35 to 40 minutes, or until bread is browned and done. Makes 1 loaf.

Mushroom Onion Bread

I had this particular recipe sitting in my files for years before I finally got around to trying it out and making any necessary changes. I only wished, after baking the bread and tasting it, that I hadn't waited so long. It is a truly delicious bread with a nice crust, one of the better breads in my files. Please read Success Tips before beginning.

1/2 pound fresh mushrooms,	1 cup skim milk crystals
cleaned and thinly sliced	1 tablespoon sugar
1 small onion, minced	2 cakes yeast
3 tablespoons butter or margarine	2 large eggs, slightly beaten
1 tablespoon salt	5 cups stirred and measured white
1-1/2 cups lukewarm water	or unbleached white flour

Before you begin making the dough, combine the mushrooms and minced onion and sauté very gently in the butter until tender. Add the salt. Cool. Do not drain. Now combine the lukewarm water, skim milk crystals, sugar, and yeast. Stir together and let proof for 5 to 8 minutes. Then stir in the eggs and 2 cups of the flour. Beat together and then add the mushrooms and onions along with the butter and pan juices they have cooked in. Stir together thoroughly and add the remaining flour, 1 cup at a time, until you have a medium dough. Turn this dough out onto a lightly floured board and knead lightly. For just a few minutes. Then rub the bread dough all over with a small amount of oil, turn it into a clean bowl, cover and let rise until double, approximately 30 to 45 minutes. When dough has doubled, punch it down and place it in a buttered 9- by 5- by 3-inch loaf pan. Cover and let rise until almost doubled this time, approximately 30 minutes. Bake in a preheated 375° F oven for 40 to 45 minutes, or until bread is browned and tests done. Makes 1 large loaf.

Cottage Cheese Bread

This recipe came from an Idaho pioneer, who just told me to mix up some powdered milk, flour, yeast and cottage cheese and it "makes a powerful good bread." And that it does, but not until I had played around with the "recipe" for a while and had worked out some of the kinks that are always in a casually given recipe of that type. I baked my finished version for a dinner party and everyone loved it. They wanted to know what gave it that distinctive texture and look, and they ate every last slice. It's the kind of bread that takes well to other flavors, so you might add some sugar, no more than 1/3 cup, and some grated orange or lemon rind for a delicately flavored bread that makes excellent toast. Another good version is to add a tablespoon or two of sesame seeds and some onion soup mix. Please read Success Tips before beginning.

1 cup skim milk crystals	1 cup cottage cheese
1 cup lukewarm water	1/4 cup salad oil, melted butter, or
1 cake yeast	margarine
2 tablespoons sugar	3 cups stirred and measured white
1-1/2 teaspoons salt	or unbleached white flour

Combine milk crystals, water and yeast. Stir together and let proof for

5 minutes. Then blend with sugar, salt, cottage cheese, salad oil and then the flour, adding the flour 1 cup at a time until you have a medium stiff dough.

Turn dough out onto a lightly floured board and knead thoroughly. This will take about 8 to 10 minutes. Then rub the dough all over with oil, turn it into a clean bowl, cover and let rise until doubled, about 1 hour.

At the end of that time, punch the dough down and turn it into a greased 9- by 5- by 3-inch bread pan or into a buttered 1-1/2 quart casserole. Cover again and let rise for a second time, this time until not quite doubled in size, approximately 45 minutes.

Bake in a preheated 375° F oven for approximately 45 minutes, or until the loaf is golden brown and tests done. Brush top with melted butter and serve hot. Makes 1 loaf.

Armenian Peda Bread

This traditional Armenian bread is one of my particular favorites. It's excellent made up into hamburger rolls, or just into loaf bread; however, the traditional flat shape lends itself well to sandwiches and provides more crust for those who enjoy crunchy bread crusts. Please read Success Tips before starting.

2 cakes yeast	5 to 6 cups stirred and measured
2 cups lukewarm water	white or unbleached white
2 tablespoons sugar	flour
2 teaspoons salt	flour glaze
2 tablespoons melted butter,	2 tablespoons sesame seeds
margarine, or lard or	
vegetable oil	

In a large bowl dissolve the yeast in 1/2 cup of the water with the sugar. Let set for several minutes, or until the yeast foams. Then add remaining water, salt, melted butter and 3 cups of the flour. Beat until it forms a smooth batter, then add remaining flour 1 cup at a time until you have a medium-firm dough.

Turn dough out onto a lightly floured bread board and knead, adding flour as necessary to keep dough from sticking. When dough is smooth and elastic turn it into a clean, greased bowl turning the dough around so that it is greased on all sides. Cover and let rise until doubled in bulk, approximately 1 hour.

When dough has risen, punch it down and divide into 2 parts. Shape each into a ball, place on a large, greased cookie sheet that has been sprinkled with flour, cover and let rest for 30 minutes.

At the end of that time press and pull and stretch each ball to shape it into a large oval that will be approximately 1/2 to 3/4 inch thick. Brush the loaves lightly with cool water. Now shape the dough: using the four fingers of each hand, press an indentation into the dough approximately 1 inch from the edge and all around, making an oval within the oval. Then, using the same method, press lines crosswise and lengthwise in the dough, within the inner oval.

Cover and allow the loaves to rise until doubled, approximately 30 to 45 minutes. Bake in a preheated 450° F oven for 15 to 20 minutes, or until loaves are browned and done.

While the loaves are rising, make the flour glaze. Combine 1/3 cup water with 1 tablespoon flour and cook and stir over medium heat until it thickens. Remove from heat, cover, and cool.

As soon as the loaves are removed from the oven, brush them all over the top and sides with the glaze. Brush twice and then sprinkle with the sesame seeds. Makes 2 loaves.

WHOLE WHEAT PEDA BREAD. Simply replace 3 cups flour with 2-1/2 cups stirred and measured whole wheat flour and 1/2 cup wheat germ.

MINIATURE LOAVES. Sometimes, for company, I make miniature loaves by dividing the dough into 6 to 8 parts and continuing as above, only of course making fewer lines across the dough.

Herb Bread

This flavorful bread can be made when convenient and the dough stored in the refrigerator overnight to be baked when needed. Please read Success Tips before beginning.

2 packages dry yeast
1/2 cup lukewarm water
2 tablespoons sugar
2/3 cup skim milk crystals
  reconstituted with
  1-3/4 cups lukewarm water
1 tablespoon salt
1/4 cup butter or margarine,
  melted; or vegetable oil

5 to 5-1/2 cups stirred and
  measured white or
  unbleached white flour
2/3 cup wheat germ
2 tablespoons minced parsley
1 tablespoon minced chives
1/2 teaspoon dried sage
1 teaspoon dried sweet basil

Combine yeast, 1/2 cup water and sugar. Let proof for 5 minutes. Then add reconstituted dry milk, salt, melted butter or oil and 2 cups of the flour. Beat until it forms a smooth batter. Add 1 more cup of flour and beat vigorously. Then stir in the wheat germ and the herbs.

Now stir in enough of the remaining flour to make a soft dough that cleans the sides of the bowl. Turn out onto a lightly floured surface and knead until the dough is smooth and elastic. Turn into a greased bowl and turn the dough so that it is greased all over. Cover and let rise until doubled in bulk, about 30 to 45 minutes.

Punch the dough down and cut into 2 parts. Shape each part into a loaf and place in a greased 8- by 4- by 2-1/2-inch loaf pan. Brush loaves with oil and cover loosely with waxed paper. Refrigerate for anywhere from 2 to 24 hours. When ready to bake, remove from refrigerator and let stand at room temperature for 10 minutes. If there are any bubbles in the loaves, prick them with a toothpick. Bake in a preheated 400° F oven for 30 to 40 minutes, or until done. Remove from pans and cool on racks. Makes 2 small loaves.

Small Butter Loaves (Petits Pains au Beurre)

Anyone who is interested in bread making at all has at least one French bread recipe and probably more. However, as Bernard Clayton, Jr. informs us in *The Breads of France*, there is a lot more to France's bread than the usual long, white or near white loaf that we are familiar with. This recipe, from his book, is excellent, and the small loaves make delicious sandwiches. If you replace the 2/3 cup light cream with 4 large egg yolks you have petits pains aux oeufs. Please read Success Tips before beginning.

Starter

1-1/3 cups milk, scalded and
    cooled to room temperature

2 cups stirred and measured white
    or unbleached white flour

2 cakes yeast

Dough

all of the starter
2/3 cup light cream or egg yolks
    (see above)
1 teaspoon salt

3 cups stirred and measured white
    flour
1/4 cup butter, at room
    temperature

For the starter, combine the scalded and cooled milk with the 2 cups flour and yeast and stir to make a thick batter. Cover with plastic wrap or a clean cloth and let stand at room temperature until the mixture ferments and bubbles, about 1-1/2 to 2 hours, or overnight if that is more convenient. The overnight fermenting will develop more flavor.

When the starter is ready to use, beat in the cream and salt and just enough of the flour to make a thick batter again. Then cut the butter into tiny chips and stir them into the batter. Now stir in the remaining flour, 1/2 cup at a time, until you have a medium but still slightly sticky dough.

Turn the dough out onto a lightly floured bread board and knead until the dough is smooth and no longer sticky, adding only enough flour as is needed. When dough has been kneaded, turn it into a clean, greased bowl and turn the dough so that it is greased all over. Cover and let the dough rise until doubled.

When dough has risen, punch it down and turn out again. Mr. Clayton suggests rolling the dough into a flat oval, cutting the oval into 4 pie-shaped pieces, making an oval of each of these pieces and cutting again, until you have 16 pieces of dough. This is, as he suggests, an accurate way of making evenly shaped loaves. However, I just cut the dough into 16 pieces and shape each piece into an oval roll that is 6 or 7 inches long. Place the rolls, seam side down, on greased cookie sheets, leaving space between the rolls for them to rise and spread. Cover the rolls and let them rise again until doubled in bulk.

Just before baking, use a razor blade to cut a slit right down the center of each roll. Bake in a preheated 400° F oven for 30 to 35 minutes, or until browned and done. Cool on racks. Makes 16 small loaves.

Raisin Bread

I have to tell you that I do not especially like raisins, but consider this possibly the best raisin bread in the world. It certainly makes the best raisin toast. The sweetening, with the exception of a little sugar, is provided by the raisins. I cover the raisins with hot water, let them set for 30 minutes, and then drain and dry the raisins. Sprinkle them with a little flour, shaking off any excess. When I make this bread for my little grandchildren I substitute a cup of wheat germ for the same amount of flour. Please read Success Tips before beginning.

2 cups evaporated milk	8 to 10 cups stirred and measured
1 cup hot water	white or unbleached white
1/3 cup sugar or honey	flour
2 cakes yeast	1 to 2 cups raisins, soaked and
2/3 cup melted lard	drained (see above)
3 large eggs	1 teaspoon orange or lemon rind
4 teaspoons salt	or vanilla extract (optional)

Combine evaporated milk, hot water and sugar. Test to make certain that the mixture is lukewarm. Stir in yeast and let it proof for 5 minutes. Then stir in the melted (but not hot) lard, the eggs, salt and 3 cups of flour. Beat until smooth. Now add the raisins, any flavoring used, and the remaining flour, 1 cup at a time, using only enough flour to make a medium dough.

Turn the dough out onto a very lightly floured board and work it lightly. It does not require much kneading at all. Turn it into a clean, greased bowl and turn the dough so that it is greased all over. Cover and let rise. When doubled in bulk, punch it down and let it rise again.

When the dough has risen twice, punch it down and turn it out onto a very lightly floured surface. Cut it into 2 or 3 pieces and shape each into a loaf, or into rolls, or however suits your fancy. Place in greased standard loaf pans — or if you have perhaps braided a large magnificent loaf, place it on a greased cookie sheet. Cover and let rise again until doubled.

When the dough is ready, bake it in a preheated 400° F oven until browned and done. This will take about 25 minutes for rolls, 45 minutes for regular loaf pans and close to an hour for a large braided loaf. The important thing is to test to make certain that the rolls or bread is done.

Buttermilk Bread

This makes a delicious, tender bread. I very often use 3/4 cup of wheat germ and 1/2 cup soy flour in place of the same amount of regular flour. Please read Success Tips before beginning.

1 quart buttermilk	2 packages yeast
1 tablespoon salt	1/2 cup lukewarm water
1/3 cup vegetable oil, butter,	1 tablespoon honey or sugar
or margarine	10 cups stirred and measured
5 tablespoons honey or sugar, or	white or unbleached white
molasses	flour

Combine the buttermilk, salt, oil, and honey in a saucepan and heat until mixture is warm. Cool to lukewarm. Dissolve the yeast in the 1/2 cup water with the 1 tablespoon honey. Let proof for 5 to 8 minutes. Then add to the cooled buttermilk mixture. Stir in 5 cups of the flour and beat until thoroughly mixed and fairly smooth. Then add remaining flour, 1 cup at a time, until it forms a medium dough.

Turn the dough out onto a lightly floured surface and knead for 8 to 10 minutes, or until dough is smooth and elastic. Then turn the dough into an oiled bowl and oil the surface of the dough all over. Cover and let rise for 45 minutes, not until doubled. Punch the dough down and, this time, let it rise until doubled in bulk, about 1 to 1-1/2 hours. Punch the dough down again and let it rise for another 45 minutes. When dough has risen the third time, punch it down and divide into 3 parts. Shape each part into a loaf and place in greased 9-inch bread pans. Cover and let rise again until doubled and then bake in a preheated 375° F oven for 45 minutes, or until the loaves are browned and test done. Makes 3 loaves.

Note: You can eliminate two of the four risings, However, the bread won't be quite as tender. The more times the dough rises until doubled in bulk, or almost doubled in bulk, the lighter and more tender the bread will be.

Cooked Cereal Bread

Old recipe books told how to use leftover cooked cereal in bread. It was practical, useful and made a good, moist bread. In recent years some cooks are again using leftover cereal to make moist, delicious breads. If you have only 1 cup of leftover cereal you will need approximately 1-1/2 cups of lukewarm water or scalded, cooled milk or its equivalent in skim milk crystals. If you have 2 cups of leftover cooked cereal decrease the amount of water or milk to 2/3 cup. Please read Success Tips before beginning.

1 or 2 cups leftover cooked cereal (see above)	1 cake yeast
2/3 to 1-1/2 cups lukewarm water or scalded, cooled milk or buttermilk (see above)	1/4 cup lukewarm water
	2 cups stirred and measured whole wheat or graham flour
2 to 4 tablespoons sugar, honey or molasses	3 to 4 cups stirred and measured white or unbleached white flour
3 tablespoons butter, margarine or lard, melted, or vegetable oil	3 tablespoons salt

Combine the leftover cereal, liquid, sugar and butter. Stir to blend well. Dissolve yeast in 1/4 cup lukewarm water and let proof for 5 to 8 minutes, or until it bubbles and rises. Add to the cereal mixture. Now beat in 1 cup of the whole-grain flour, 2 cups of the white flour and the salt. Beat thoroughly and then add remaining flour, 1 cup at a time, until you have a medium dough which can be kneaded without stickiness.

Turn the dough out onto a very lightly floured board and knead until smooth and elastic. Place in a greased bowl and turn the dough so that it is greased all over. Cover and let rise until doubled in bulk. When double, punch it down and shape into 2 loaves. Place in greased 8-inch loaf pans, cover and let rise until doubled in bulk again. Bake in a preheated 375° F oven for 35 to 45 minutes, or until browned and done. Makes 2 loaves.

Lettuce Bread

I know exactly what you're going to say. "Lettuce in bread! It sounds crazy!" Exactly what you would have said ten years ago at the idea of putting grated zucchini in bread. Take my word for it, this is a delicately flavored, slightly lemony loaf. The bright green shreds of lettuce stay green, giving the baked loaf a speckled look, as well as added moisture. The flavor is luscious. As with any bread of this type, don't overmix the batter.

2 cups sugar	1/4 teaspoon cinnamon
1 cup vegetable oil	1/4 teaspoon powdered ginger
4 large eggs	3 cups stirred and measured white
4 teaspoons baking powder	or unbleached white flour
1 teaspoon baking soda	1 tablespoon fresh lemon juice
1 teaspoon salt	2 cups finely chopped lettuce

1 cup chopped walnuts

Beat the sugar with the oil and eggs. Stir the baking powder, soda, salt, spices and flour together and add to the oil mixture. Then stir in the lemon juice and lettuce and nuts. Turn the batter into a well-greased 9-inch loaf pan and bake in a preheated 350° F oven for 1 hour and 30 minutes. Test the loaf carefully with a cake tester or wooden pick to make certain that it is done in the center. Turn out onto a rack to cool. Cool several hours before cutting. Makes 1 loaf.

Beer Bread

There are fads in food just as there are in everything else. I remember when everyone was making wacky cake, a chocolate cake that was mixed right in the pan it was baked in. Then there was monkey bread, baked in layers that could be pulled apart. A few years ago we all made our own liqueurs with fresh fruit, rock candy and vodka. Then there was zucchini bread and potato chip cookies. This year's fad is Beer Bread, quickly and easily made and delicious.

3 cups stirred and measured	2 tablespoons sugar
self-rising flour	1 12-ounce can beer
(See page 38.)	1/2 cup butter or
	margarine, melted

Combine flour and sugar and mix with a spoon to blend. Add beer a third at a time, stirring it in. Turn into a greased 9- by 5-inch loaf pan and drizzle the melted butter over the top. Let the loaf set for 10 minutes before baking in a preheated 375° F oven for 50 minutes to an hour, or until done.

BEER ROLLS. Mix as directed above, only turn into greased muffin tins. Pour melted butter over and bake in a preheated 400° F oven for 20 minutes, or until done.

Ann Larson's Sauerkraut Bread

Ann Larson is my partner in catering. An exquisite cook who serves food that is as beautiful to look at as it is to eat, she claims this is one of her favorite snack breads.

3/4 cup drained sauerkraut	1-1/2 teaspoons sugar
3 tablespoons butter	dash pepper
1/4 cup sliced green onions	1/4 teaspoon salt
1/2 cup shredded carrots	2 tablespoons parsley
1/2 teaspoon caraway seeds	2 cups Biscuit Mix (see page 27.)

Herb Butter

Place the drained sauerkraut on several layers of paper toweling. Press to remove as much moisture as possible. Melt butter in a large skillet; sauté green onions, carrots, and sauerkraut for 5 minutes, stirring occasionally. Remove from heat and stir in the caraway seeds, sugar, pepper, salt, and parsley. In a bowl combine the Biscuit Mix and enough milk to make a workable dough. Turn dough onto lightly floured bread board and knead it lightly just 4 or 5 times.

Roll the dough out into a rectangle about 12 by 16 inches. Sprinkle the sauerkraut mixture over the dough and roll the dough, jelly-roll fashion, beginning with the long end. Shape into a horseshoe on a greased cookie sheet. Tuck the ends under so that the filling is not exposed. Brush with beaten egg and sprinkle with more caraway seeds. Bake in a preheated 375° F oven for 30 to 35 minutes, or until browned and done. Serve warm with Herb Butter.

Herb Butter

Combine 1 cup butter or margarine, 1/4 teaspoon caraway seed, 1/8 teaspoon thyme leaves and 1/8 teaspoon marjoram. Beat with a mixer and let stand for at least 1 hour before using.

Zucchini Bread

A hundred years ago there were only few basic breads, the housewife made and varied them as she could. For example, this old recipe for a dried fruit bread was sent to me by a reader, "Make bread dough as usual. Set aside enough dough for 1 loaf. Cook 1 cup dried prunes and dried apple with 2 tablespoons sugar and a dash of spice and enough water to keep from burning, until tender. Run through grinder. Mix with the set-aside dough and add enough flour to handle. Let raise and bake as usual." Now new recipes for assorted kinds of breads are available almost monthly in the magazines. And one of the latest bread fads is Zucchini Bread.

There are many recipes for Zucchini Bread. Some cooks change the seasonings, and some add pineapple or grated carrots. However, the basic recipes are the same, beginning with 3 or 4 eggs and a cup of light vegetable oil. Be sure to read Success Tips before beginning and remember to blend the mixture *gently* so that you do not crush the zucchini shreds while mixing. If you crush the shreds too much, the mixture will be too wet to bake properly.

3 large eggs	3 cups stirred and measured white
1 cup light vegetable oil	or unbleached white flour
3/4 to 1 cup each: granulated	2 teaspoons each baking soda and
sugar and brown sugar	salt
1 tablespoon flavoring	1/2 teaspoon baking powder
(see below)	1 cup chopped walnuts
2 cups coarsely shredded raw	1/3 cup chopped raisins or
zucchini	sesame seeds

Beat the eggs to blend. Add the oil, sugar and flavoring and beat until mixture is thick and foamy. Stir in the zucchini carefully. Combine dry ingredients and gently stir into the mixture just until blended.

Divide batter between 2 buttered and floured 9- by 5-inch loaf pans. You can sprinkle a few more chopped walnuts or sesame seeds over the top. Let set for 10 minutes before baking in a preheated 350° F oven for 1 hour, or until bread tests done when a pick is stuck through the middle. Cool in pans for 10 minutes, then turn out onto wire racks to cool thoroughly.

PINEAPPLE ZUCCHINI BREAD. Follow basic recipe, and add an 8-ounce can of well-drained crushed pineapple.

FLAVORINGS. You can add 2 teaspoons maple flavoring or vanilla extract, or 1 teaspoon of each. Some good cooks use a tablespoon of cinnamon combined with 2 or 3 teaspoons vanilla, or a tablespoon of grated lemon rind.

OTHER VARIATIONS. Many good cooks use 1 cup of chopped raisins or dates instead of 1/3 cup raisins or sesame. And some use 1 cup whole wheat flour in place of the same amount of white flour. Others replace 1/2 cup of flour with the same amount of wheat germ. All variations are good. And the bread freezes well.

APPLE BREAD. Follow the recipe for Zucchini Bread. In place of the zucchini, shred or grate 3 or 4 peeled and cored tart apples, to make a total of 2 cups fruit. Stir 1 or 2 teaspoons of lemon juice into the apples to keep them white.

ORANGE BREAD. Follow the recipe for Zucchini Bread. In place of zucchini, you will need 3 or 4 fairly large oranges to make the necessary 2 cups of pulp. First grate the peel so that you have 2 tablespoons grated peel. Then peel the oranges and remove the white pith. Remove the seeds and then chop enough pulp to make 2 cups.

GREEN TOMATO BREAD. Follow the recipe for Zucchini Bread. In place of the zucchini, use 2 cups coarsely chopped green tomatoes.

Orange Marmalade Nut Bread

This bread, another from fellow caterer Ann Larson, gets its flavor from orange marmalade combined with orange juice, and its moist quality from mashed potato. Please read Success Tips before beginning.

1/2 cup butter or margarine	4-1/2 cups stirred and measured
2 tablespoons vegetable	unbleached white or white
shortening (you could use	flour
the same amount of butter)	4-1/2 teaspoons baking powder
1 cup sugar	1 teaspoon baking soda
2 large eggs	1 teaspoon salt
3 tablespoons organge marmalade	1 cup orange juice
1 small potato, cooked and	1 cup chopped pecans, walnuts, or
mashed	slivered almonds

Cream the butter and shortening thoroughly. Gradually beat in the sugar, beating until mixture is light and fluffy. Beat in the eggs, marmalade and mashed potato. Sift dry ingredients and add to the beaten mixture alternately with the orange juice. Stir 1 teaspoon of flour through the nuts and shake so that any excess flour is discarded. Fold into the batter and pour into 2 well-greased 8-inch loaf pans. Cover with foil and bake in a preheated 350° F oven for 20 minutes, remove the foil and continue baking for another 30 to 40 minutes, or until the crust is golden and the bread tests done.

Remove to racks and cook for 15 minutes, then turn out of pans and continue cooling. Makes 2 small loaves.

Lemon and Lime Nut Bread

This good nut bread uses a lemon and lime carbonated beverage for part of its flavor. Remember that in breads of this type you mix only enough to moisten the ingredients. *Do not beat.*

2-1/2 cups stirred and measured white or unbleached white flour
1 tablespoon baking powder
1 teaspoon salt
2/3 cup sugar
1 cup chopped walnuts or mixed nuts
1 tablespoon grated fresh lemon rind
1 tablespoon grated fresh lime rind
1 large egg, beaten
1 cup lemon and lime carbonated beverage
2 tablespoons vegetable oil

Combine flour, baking powder, salt, and sugar. Stir together and then add the nuts and grated rinds. Stir to mix. Combine liquid ingredients and beat together just to blend. Add, all at once, to the dry ingredients, stirring together just enough so that mixture is thoroughly moistened and there are no dry spots. Spoon batter into a well-greased 9-inch loaf pan. Let stand for 10 minutes before baking. Then bake in a preheated 350° F oven for 45 minutes, or until bread tests done. Cool on a rack.

Note. For a touch of glamor, sprinkle the top of the bread with a mixture of 2 tablespoons each of grated fresh lemon rind and sugar. Sprinkle this on the bread 10 minutes before it is done. Makes 1 loaf.

Lemon Nut Bread

This piquantly flavored quick bread has been making the rounds for years. It's perfect with tea or coffee and is especially good when spread with slightly lemon-flavored whipped cream cheese. *Some recipes use milk in place of buttermilk, in which case the only adjustment that needs be made is to omit the baking soda.* This is a good recipe for use with the food processor. Be sure to read Success Tips before beginning.

1 cup walnuts or pecans
1 large lemon
1 cup sugar
1/2 cup butter or margarine, cut into chunks
2 cups stirred and measured white or unbleached white flour
2 teaspoons baking powder
1 teaspoon baking soda
1/2 teaspoon salt
1/2 cup buttermilk
2 large eggs

Glaze

1/3 cup freshly squeezed lemon juice
1/2 cup sugar

Chop the walnuts in the food processor with quick off and on motions and set them aside. Cut the zest from the lemon with a sharp knife and put in the processor container with the sugar. Process until the peel is grated and you have a fine lemon-sugar. Add the butter and cream until light and fluffy. Stir together the dry ingredients and add half to the container, processing very briefly. Add the buttermilk and eggs and process only until the flour is moistened. Do not over-process.

Add the nuts and stir together just to mix. Turn batter into a greased 9- by 5-inch loaf pan that has been lined with waxed paper and greased again. Let sit for 15 minutes and then bake in a preheated 375° F oven for 50 to 60 minutes, or until a cake tester or toothpick comes out clean. Do not overbake.

Cool on a rack, in the pan, while you make the glaze.

Stir together the lemon juice and sugar and heat until the sugar dissolves. Pierce the hot loaf of bread all over deeply with a cake tester or toothpick and pour the hot liquid over the hot loaf. Let the loaf sit for 30 or 40 minutes before turning out of the pan. The loaf should still be warm so that the waxed paper will peel off easily.

Note. Cooled thoroughly and then completely wrapped in foil, the bread will keep for several weeks in the refrigerator, or for 3 or 4 months in the freezer. Little sandwiches made with thin slices of the bread and whipped cream cheese, wrapped in foil, will keep for 2 or 3 days in the refrigerator.

ORANGE NUT BREAD. Follow recipe above, substituting 1/4 cup grated orange rind for the lemon rind and make the glaze with a mixture of 1/3 cup fresh orange juice and 1/3 cup Triple Sec or other orange flavored liqueur. Don't heat the glaze, just pour over a pierced hot loaf.

PIZZA TYPE BREADS

Almost the whole western world loves pizza. We have American and Italian variations of the Italian dish; the Lebanese *sfeeha*, a meatcake which is made by Armenians also; the German *zwiebelkuchen*; and some people would include the French *quiche*, especially in its original form, with a bread base rather than with a pastry base.

Foccacia (page 74) was probably the forerunner of pizza as we know it today. A piece of dough, spread out and covered with whatever happened to be at hand. Some tomato and cheese, or simply a drizzle of olive oil and some garlic. Eaten fresh from the oven, it's good regardless.

The bread plates and pizza stones that are sold throughout the country are excellent. They aid in the making of a superior crust, and are fun to use. However, I still use the aluminum pizza pans that I bought when my children were small. I spread the pans with oil, sprinkle with some corn meal, and make certain that the dough has "rested" for 10 to 15 minutes before spreading it out. In this way, the dough is "relaxed" enough to spread out without springing back. It saves the frustration of seeing a 12-inch circle of dough shrink to a 6-inch circle before your eyes.

You can bake your pizza on just about anything that will take the heat and fit into your oven — or on top of your stove. When my oven went out while I was making a pizza for my sons, I simply fried it. I rolled the dough out and placed it in a hot, lightly greased skillet. I cooked it until it was done on one side, then turned it over, spread the top with the usual pizza makings, and continued cooking it until it was done. It was very good, with a deliciously crisp crust. Now, when someone wants a pizza, and I don't want to heat the oven for *one*, I cook it on top of the stove.

Today's imaginative, innovative cooks have come up with a limitless array of pizzas, some good, some marvelous, and some, unfortunately, atrocious. I know a woman who makes a type of pizza with a rye crust and spreads it with ham and cheese. It's different, and it's good, but I don't know that I'd call it pizza. Another cook I know came up with a pizza combining ham, cheese, green pepper and pineapple. I never could manage to eat any of it.

Pizza Crust

Although I gave a special recipe for the crust in my first book, *A World of Breads*, and will give two in this book, I have always found that almost any yeast dough, especially with the addition of a generous amount of cracked black pepper, will make a good crust—*as long as it is thin*, for a regular pizza. Your thick-crusted pizza is another matter entirely. What you want is *either* a thin-crusted pizza, *or* a deep-pan pizza. Not something that is in between, and therefore neither. Sourdough makes an excellent crust for pizza, as does a good whole wheat bread dough, although neither is traditional by any means. I've even used a *brioche* dough that I had in my freezer, and with good results.

Pizza freezes very well. And if yours is a pizza-loving family, it would certainly be worth your while to make, and freeze, an extra pizza each time you make it. Using ingredients that are at room temperature, make your pizza as usual, *only do not bake it.* Wrap and freeze. When ready to use it remove wrappings and bake the pizza, *unthawed,* in a preheated 500° F degree oven for 30 minutes, or until done.

Thick-Crusted Pizza Dough

This type of pizza has become increasingly popular in recent years. *The dough can be prepared through the first rising, and then punched down and wrapped securely and frozen. When ready to use, thaw and let dough rise until doubled in bulk, divide into 2 or 3 parts, add filling, and bake as directed.*

2-1/2 cups lukewarm water	1 package active dry yeast
1/2 cup vegetable or olive oil	dissolved in 1/4 cup
8 cups stirred and measured white	lukewarm water
or unbleached white	2 teaspoons salt
flour	1 to 2 tablespoons coarsely ground
1/2 cup yellow corn meal	black pepper

4 large eggs
additional oil and corn meal

Combine water and oil. Stir in 4 cups of the flour, the corn meal, dissolved yeast, salt, pepper and eggs. Beat thoroughly until smooth. Now add remaining flour, 1 cup at a time, using just enough to make a dough that is easily handled.

Turn the dough out onto a lightly floured surface and knead until smooth and elastic, about 5 to 8 minutes. Turn the kneaded dough into an oiled bowl, turning dough so that it is oiled all over. Cover and let rise until doubled in bulk, about 1-1/2 hours.

When dough has doubled in bulk, punch it down and divide into 2 or 3 parts, depending on just how thick you want the pizza to be. Place each part in an oiled and corn meal-sprinkled 9- by 13-inch pan.

Let rest for 10 minutes and then spread the dough out, making a rim. You are now ready to add the filling.

Sprinkle the dough with sliced cooked Italian sausage and some cooked mushrooms and green peppers. Grate enough mozzarella, Scamorze, or Jack cheese to make a thick layer. Spread with a good sauce, either homemade or canned. Sprinkle with crumbled oregano and a little more cheese. Then sprinkle with some grated Parmesan or Romano and bake immediately, without letting the dough rise again, in a preheated 375° F to 400° F oven until the crust is brown and the cheese is melted. This will take approximately 30 minutes.

Note. This recipe will also make 2 loaves of very good bread. Simply make as directed, adding 2 teaspoons of crushed dried rosemary if desired. After the first rising, place dough in 2 greased 9-inch loaf pans. Let rise again and bake in a preheated 375° F oven until browned and done, approximately 40 to 45 minutes.

Thin-Crusted Pizza Dough

As stated in the foreward to this section, any bread dough can be used as the crust for pizza. Naturally, a simple dough that would make a firm, crisp crust is most desirable. The following recipe is excellent.

1 package active dry yeast	1 teaspoon salt
1-1/2 cups lukewarm water	1 tablespoon coarsely ground
3-1/2 to 4 cups stirred and	black pepper
measured white or	2 tablespoons vegetable or olive
unbleached white flour	oil

additional oil and some corn meal

Dissolve the yeast in the water and let it proof for 5 to 8 minutes. Then stir in 3 cups of the flour, the salt, pepper, and oil. Beat until smooth. Then add remaining flour gradually until you have a firm dough. Knead the dough lightly and turn it into an oiled bowl. Turn the dough so that the surface is oiled all over. Cover and let rise until doubled, 1 to 1-1/2 hours.

When dough has doubled in bulk, punch it down and cut in two. Place each part on an oiled and corn meal-sprinkled 12-inch pizza pan. Let the dough rest for 10 minutes and then spread it out so that it covers the pan. Make your pizza according to your favorite recipe and bake immediately in a preheated 500° F oven until the crusts are crisp and done. This will take about 20 to 25 minutes.

Italian Onion Bread (Focaccia)

This is a thin, crusty snack bread, superb by itself or with meals. I serve a bread like this — with the onions — with a casual buffet of spaghetti and salad, or with barbecued meat or poultry. If you don't have a food processor just make the dough as you would for any simple bread.

5 to 6 cups stirred and measured white or unbleached white flour

2 packages dry yeast, dissolved in 1 cup lukewarm water

1/4 cup olive or vegetable oil
1 teaspoon sugar
2 teaspoons salt
1 egg yolk beaten with 2 tablespoons milk or cream, for glaze

Topping

3 large onions, minced
1 or 2 cloves garlic, crushed

2 tablespoons olive or vegetable oil

freshly ground black pepper

Using the food processor, with the metal blade in place, turn 3 cups of the flour into the bowl. Add remaining dough ingredients, *not the remaining flour.* Turn food processor on and off rapidly until a batter is formed. Add 1 more cup flour and process until it forms a heavy dough.

Turn the remaining cup of flour onto a clean surface and add the dough from the processor. Knead the dough, adding as much flour as can be incorporated into the dough. It won't require much kneading as most of the work has been done by the processor. Place dough in an oiled or greased bowl and turn the dough so that it is completely spread with a thin film of oil. Cover and let rise until doubled in bulk, approximately 1 hour.

In the meantime, sauté the onions and garlic in the oil, just until soft.

When the dough has risen, cut it in half and knead again for a few minutes. Now cut each half into 3 pieces and let rest for 10 minutes. Then roll each piece into a rectangle about 6 by 10 inches. The edges of the rectangle should be slightly raised. Brush with beaten egg yolk and spread with sautéed onions, then sprinkle with freshly ground black pepper. Bake several at a time, on a greased cookie sheet, in a preheated 400° F oven for 15 to 20 minutes, or until browned and done. You will have to check often as the baking time is really determined by the thickness of the dough.

TOMATO FOCACCIA. Place dough in a greased 9- by 13-inch shallow pan. Let it rise until almost, but not quite, doubled. Punch holes all over the dough and spread with a highly seasoned thickened tomato sauce. Sprinkle with a mixture of grated Romano or Parmesan cheese and some crushed garlic. Bake immediately in a preheated 375° F oven until done. Cut and serve hot.

SAGE OR ROSEMARY FOCACCIA. This makes a deliciously fragrant bread. The sage is not too much, and lends a delightful flavor. If you have any of this bread left over, simply dry it and save for stuffing mixtures. Make the dough as directed, adding 2 or 3 teaspoons of dried sage leaves *or* the same amount of dried rosemary to the dough. Omit onion topping and brush surface of the bread with some olive oil before baking.

Calzone

Calzone is a version of the popular pizza. It varies from cook to cook, with some making the calzone into small turnovers, large turnovers, a pie, or even rolling the dough around the filling, jelly-roll style.

Some deep fry the calzone but we much prefer it baked. When my children were in school, I would serve the turnovers with soup and salad for a hearty lunch. Now I serve them with barbecues and find that people enjoy their appealingly different flavor.

This basic recipe is especially easy with the food processor. Work your way right through the recipe, first grating the cheese and setting it aside. Then chop the onions and set them on to cook, then chop the tomatoes (if you use fresh), and add the olives last as you don't want them ground, just chopped. After adding that to the onions, I rinse out the processor and make the dough. The whole procedure takes only a few mintues. But make the dough last, as the processor bowl must then be relegated to the dishwasher.

Filling

2 medium-sized onions, peeled and cut into quarters	1 cup pitted black olives
	1 cup pitted green olives
2 tablespoons vegetable or olive oil	1/2 cup fresh parsley
	1 cup grated Romano or Parmesan cheese
5 fresh tomatoes, cored	

Dough

2 cakes yeast	1 teaspoon salt
3/4 cup lukewarm water	2 tablespoons vegetable or olive oil
3 cups stirred and measured white or unbleached white flour	1/2 cup water

Chop the onions in the food processor bowl with a quick on and off motion. Turn them into a frying pan with the oil and sauté just until golden. Add the tomatoes, olives, and parsley that have been chopped in the food processor. Simmer, uncovered, for 15 to 20 minutes. Then add the cheese and remove from heat.

Combine yeast and water in food processor bowl. Let stand for 5 minutes, then add remaining ingredients for the dough. Turn the processor on and off rapidly until the dough forms a ball around the metal blade.

Turn the dough into a clean, greased bowl and turn the dough around so that it is greased all over. Cover and let rise until double in bulk, approximately 45 minutes.

When the dough has doubled, turn it out onto a lightly floured bread board and roll it out into a large rectangle. Cut into 8 square pieces. Place some of the filling just off center of each square of dough. Fold the top over like a turnover and seal the edges with a bit of water so that they stick. If you want you might brush the tops with beaten egg and sprinkle with sesame seeds. Bake immediately in a preheated 400° F oven for 20 minutes, or until tops are browned and done. Makes 8.

VARIATIONS. You can use a filling of chopped sautéed onions topped with a layer of sliced ripe olives. Another traditional and delicious filling uses 1-1/2 pounds ricotta, 1/2 to 3/4 cup chopped Italian or American ham, 1/4 cup grated Romano or Parmesan cheese, 2 eggs, salt and pepper to taste, and a bit of chopped parsley. I sometimes use the basic tomato filling and add some cooked, chopped Italian sausage.

Sfeeha

This is the perfect recipe for these delicious Lebanese meat cakes. On the West Coast they can be bought at food stands and in many Armenian or Middle Eastern markets. Wherever they are sold they rival pizza in popularity.

Dough

2 cakes yeast dissolved in 2 cups lukewarm water	6 to 7 cups stirred and measured white or unbleached white
1 teaspoon honey or sugar	flour

2 teaspoons salt
1/4 cup vegetable or olive oil

Add honey to yeast mixture. Proof for 5 to 8 minutes. Then stir in 4 cups of the flour, the salt, and oil. Beat until smooth and then add remaining flour, 1 cup at a time, until you have a smooth, medium dough. Turn out onto a lightly floured surface and knead for 5 minutes. Then turn dough into an oiled bowl and rub the surface of the dough with oil. Cover and let rise until doubled in bulk, about 45 minutes to an hour. While the dough is rising, prepare the filling.

Filling

2 pounds onions, minced and sautéed just until golden in a little oil	1 small can tomato paste
	1/2 to 3/4 cup minced fresh parsley
3-1/2 pounds lean ground lamb (beef may be substituted in all or part; however, it will not give the same taste as the lamb, and will not be as good,	1/3 cup fresh lemon juice
	1-1/2 teaspoons salt
	1 teaspoon coarsely ground black pepper
	1 or 2 teaspoons cinnamon

Add the lamb to the drained onion, along with the remaining ingredients. Do not cook any further. Mix together thoroughly and set aside.

When the dough has risen, punch it down and divide into 20 small balls. Cover these and let them set for 10 minutes. Then, using a rolling pin, roll out a few at a time. They should be thin. Place on ungreased cookie sheets and spread, right to the edges, with filling. Bake immediately in a preheated 450°F to 475°F oven for 8 to 10 minutes. When finished, the meat cakes should be pale, *not* browned. Cool on racks. You will probably only be able to bake 2 or 3 at a time, but keep going, because they freeze beautifully. Use 2 cookie sheets and have one ready to go into the oven as soon as one is removed.

VARIATION. The tomato paste can be omitted, in which case you would use a little more lemon juice and some pine nuts. Bake as directed. I very often omit the tomato paste and use some seeded, diced, fresh tomatoes—about 2 or 3, depending on size.

TO FREEZE. When the cakes have cooled, stack them, meat side together, wrap carefully, and freeze. I wrap 6 of them in a package, 2 on 2 with the filling together. To reheat, place, meat side up, on cookie sheets. Sprinkle with a little grated Jack cheese if desired and heat, uncovered, in a 425° F oven for 5 minutes. Makes 20 large cakes.

Tomato-Cheese Bread

This pizza-type bread is easy to make and delicious. Serve it as part of a light supper or for the crew when they're watching television.

1 cup Biscuit Mix (see page 27)	1/4 cup mayonnaise
1/3 cup milk	1/2 cup grated Cheddar cheese
2 tomatoes, seeded and sliced	1/4 teaspoon salt
1 onion, minced	dash of coarsely ground black
1 tablespoon vegetable or olive oil	pepper
1/3 cup sour cream	1/4 teaspoon oregano
	dash thyme

Combine Biscuit Mix and milk to make a soft dough. Turn the dough out onto a floured surface and knead very lightly, just enough so that the mixture holds together. Then pat the dough over the bottom and sides of a greased 8-inch square baking pan, making a rim to hold in the filling.

Arrange tomatoes over the dough. Sauté the onion in the oil until golden. Add remaining ingredients to onions and stir together. Spoon mixture over the tomatoes. Sprinkle with a little more oregano if desired and bake in a preheated 400°F oven for 20 to 25 minutes, or until done. Let stand for 10 minutes before cutting and serving. Serves 6.

Pizza Bread

This different bread has all the flavor of pizza except the sausage. It's fun to make and serve and is good besides. Please read Success Tips before beginning.

2 cakes yeast
1-1/2 cups lukewarm water
1 teaspoon honey or sugar
2 tablespoons vegetable or olive oil
3 cups stirred and measured white or unbleached white flour
1 cup stirred and measured whole wheat flour

1 cup grated Parmesan or Romano cheese
1/2 to 1 cup minced ripe olives, drained
3 to 4 teaspoons garlic salt
2 teaspoons sweet basil
2 teaspoons oregano
1 teaspoon chili powder

Dissolve yeast in the water. Add the honey and let the yeast proof for 5 to 8 minutes. Add the oil, 2 cups of the white flour and all of the remaining ingredients. Beat thoroughly and add just enough of the remaining flour to make a firm dough. Turn the dough out onto a lightly floured surface and knead thoroughly. Add a little more flour if needed to prevent sticking. When dough has been kneaded, turn it into an oiled bowl and oil the surface of the dough. Cover and let rise until doubled, about 1 to 1-1/2 hours.

When the dough has doubled in bulk, punch it down and shape it into 1 or 2 long narrow loaves. Place loaves on a greased, lightly corn mealed baking sheet. Cover and let rise until almost, but not quite, doubled in bulk, about 45 to 50 minutes. Bake in a preheated 350° F oven until loaves are browned and test done, about 50 minutes to an hour. Makes 1 or 2 loaves, depending on size.

Navajo Tacos

This is a delicous recipe from the southwest. I ate these tacos several times, loved them, and finally came up with this approximation. The teens in the family will love them and they make good casual company fare.

Filling

1 pound lean ground beef	2 large cans pinto beans
1 large onion, minced	(28-ounce size)
2 cloves garlic, minced	3 tablespoons chili powder

salt and pepper to taste

Indian Fry Bread

3 cups stirred and measured white	1/2 teaspoon salt
or unbleached white flour	1/3 cup lard
2 tablespoons baking powder	2/3 cup warm water

oil for frying

Topping

shredded lettuce	diced tomatoes
shredded Cheddar cheese	diced California green chilis
diced onion	(optional)

First make the filling. Brown the beef with the onion and garlic, stirring frequently. Set aside. Combine the beans and chili powder and add salt and pepper to taste. Heat thoroughly and then add the meat mixture and simmer together.

Make the Fry Bread as follows: Combine dry ingredients. Cut in the lard until mixture is crumbly. Gradually add the water, using only enough so that the dough sticks together. Knead the dough lightly and divide into 10 balls. Cover the balls of dough and let them rest for 15 minutes, then pat out until they are like large, thin pancakes. Fry, one at a time, in hot oil to cover. Turn once. Drain on paper towels and keep warm.

Arrange the topping ingredients on a platter. To serve, place a round of bread on each plate and spread liberally with the filling mixture. Pass the platter of lettuce, cheese, onion, tomato and green chili.

Note. If you wish, you can add a spoonful of quacamole to the top of each. Serves 5 or more.

ROLLS, MUFFINS, AND BISCUITS

Onion Bagels

A venerable Jewish gentleman once told me that the bagels made from my recipe in *A World of Breads* were the best he had ever tasted.

These are just as good. The unique crust and texture of the bagel is achieved by dipping the bagels into boiling water before baking. Bagels are best eaten fresh, but they do freeze well. If you freeze them, reheat them before serving. Please read Success Tips before beginning.

1/2 cup instant minced onion
1 cake yeast dissolved in 2 cups
    lukewarm water
2 tablespoons sugar
1 tablespoon salt

6-1/2 cups stirred and measured
    white or unbleached white
    flour
1/4 cup poppy seeds or caraway
    seeds or a mixture of the two

3 to 4 quarts boiling water with
1 tablespoon salt added

Toast the onion in a dry, heavy iron skillet over medium heat until it just changes color. Do not let the onion burn. Set aside.

Add sugar and salt to the dissolved yeast with 4 cups of the flour. Beat thoroughly. Then stir in the onion and the seeds and enough of the remaining flour to make a firm dough. Turn the dough out into a floured surface and knead, adding a little more flour if necessary. Turn dough into an oiled bowl and oil the surface of the dough. Cover and let rise until doubled in bulk. Punch the dough down and turn it out onto a floured surface again. Pinch off pieces of dough and roll the dough pieces between the palms of the hand to make ropes of dough about 6 inches long. Pinch the ends together to make doughnut shapes. Seal the ends together and let rise again.

Dissolve the salt in the boiling water. Very carefully drop in 3 or 4 bagels at a time. They should not be crowded. Let boil for 3 minutes, turning over several times. Remove bagels to a greased baking sheet and continue until all have been boiled. Bake in a preheated 425° F oven for 25 minutes, or until browned and done.

WHOLE WHEAT BAGELS. Substitute honey for sugar, and use 2 cups whole wheat or graham flour in place of as much white flour. To make an interesting Pumpernickel Bagel use 2 cups each of rye and whole wheat flour in place of as much white flour and substitute molasses for the sugar.

Basic Sweet Dough

I almost hate to term "basic" something so rich and delicious.

However, this dough is basic in the sense that with it you can make a variety of sweet rolls and coffeecakes that will be limited only by the limits of your own imagination. I occasionally take 1/3 of the dough and mix candied fruits and chopped nuts into it, bake the dough in a Bundt pan or angel cake pan and, when baked, drizzle it with a thick glaze. I use it as the basis for fruit *kuchens,* and occasionally use it for doughnuts. The recipe as given is a large one, but is easily cut in half if desired.

I make the full amount of dough, bake it as desired, and freeze the baked goodies so as to have a sweet ready whenever needed. The dough is rich, and thus will keep well in the refrigerator for several days if you can't bake all of it at once. Please read Success Tips before beginning.

4 cakes yeast	1 tablespoon salt
1/2 cup lukewarm water	1 cup butter or margarine,
3 cups evaporated milk (do not use	softened
any other milk, although you	8 large eggs plus an additional
could use cream)	4 egg yolks
1 cup sugar	12 to 14 cups stirred and measured
1/4 cup grated lemon or orange	white or unbleached white
rind (optional)	flour

Dissolve yeast in lukewarm water and let proof for 5 to 8 minutes. Combine evaporated milk, sugar, lemon rind, salt, and butter and heat until barely lukewarm and butter has melted. Pour into large mixing bowl. Add the yeast and eggs, *first making certain that milk mixture is barely lukewarm so that you don't kill the yeast and cook the eggs.* Add 6 cups of the flour and beat thoroughly, until you have a smooth batter. Then stir in remaining flour, 1 cup at a time, adding only enough to make a medium dough that pulls away from the sides of the bowl. Rub it all over with a little oil, cover and let rise until doubled in bulk. *No kneading is necessary.*

When dough has doubled, punch it down and shape and bake it as desired, letting it rise again until doubled before baking.

CINNAMON ROLLS. Use half of recipe and divide dough into 2 parts. Roll each part out into a rectangle, brush with melted butter and sprinkle liberally with cinnamon and with brown sugar and raisins or currants, or chopped candied fruit, and chopped walnuts or pecans. You should use approximately 1 pound brown sugar, 2 cups raisins and 1 to 2 cups nuts for the 2 rolls. Roll up jelly-roll fashion and cut into 1-inch slices. Place the slices, cut side down, in greased muffin tins that have had a spoonful of honey and some chopped nuts and a bit more brown sugar placed in the bottom of each. Cover and let rise until doubled and bake in a preheated 375° F oven for 20 to 25 minutes, or until browned and done. Makes approximately 4 dozen.

COFFEECAKE. Use half of recipe and divide dough into 2 parts. Roll each into a rectangle and brush lightly with melted butter. Sprinkle liberally with chopped walnuts or pecans, brown sugar, cinnamon and some chopped dates, raisins, chopped dried figs, or other dried fruit or candied fruit. Roll up tightly as for a jelly roll and place each roll in a well-greased bread pan. Cover and let rise until doubled in bulk and then bake in a preheated 350° F oven for about 45 minutes, or until browned and the loaf tests done. Cool on racks and then drizzle with a powdered sugar glaze.

Romano Herb Batter Rolls

These hearty rolls will give any lunch or dinner a lift. And they are simple to make, taking no more than 2 hours from start to finish. This recipe is made according to the RapidMix method. Please read Success Tips before beginning.

3-1/4 cups stirred and measured white or unbleached white flour	2 tablespoons sugar
	2 teaspoons salt
	1 large egg
2 packages dry yeast	1 cup grated Romano or Parmesan
1/2 cup milk	cheese mixed with
1/2 cup water	1/2 teaspoon each:
1/2 cup butter, margarine or	dried oregano and marjoram
vegetable oil	vegetable oil
sesame or poppy seeds	

Stir together 1 cup of the flour and the yeast. Heat milk, water, butter, sugar, and salt until warm. Add all at once to the flour-yeast mixture and beat until smooth using an electric mixer.

Blend in the egg, 1 more cup of flour and the cheese-herb mixture. Beat with electric mixer for another 2 minutes. Then stir in the remaining flour to make a thick batter. Stir together thoroughly, cover and let rise for 1 hour, or until doubled. Stir down and then drop by spoonfuls into greased muffin tins. Brush with the oil and sprinkle with seeds. Cover and let rise for 30 minutes, or until doubled. Bake in a preheated 350° F oven for approximately 20 to 25 minutes, or until golden brown and done. Makes approximately 18.

Hard Dinner Rolls (Kaiser Rolls)

These delicious rolls are as close to the traditional Kaiser roll as I have been able to get. I shape them into plain round rolls, having never mastered the traditional Kaiser roll shape. I'll give instructions for shaping the rolls traditionally, however, and if you master the technique, let me know how. *To make a good, firm roll you need a good, high-protein unbleached flour. Since this is hard to buy in many areas, you can use a regular all-purpose flour as long as you substitute 1 cup gluten flour (available in any health food store) for 1 cup of the all-purpose flour.* Please read Success Tips before beginning.

1 cake yeast	1 egg, beaten
1/2 cup lukewarm water	5 to 5-1/2 cups stirred and
1 tablespoon sugar	measured white or
1-1/2 cups lukewarm water	unbleached white flour
2 teaspoons salt	(See above)

Dissolve yeast in 1/2 cup lukewarm water with the sugar. Let proof for 5 minutes. Then add remaining water, salt, egg and 4 cups of the flour. Beat together thoroughly. Add just enough of the remaining flour to make a firm dough.

Turn dough out on a lightly floured bread board and knead thoroughly, using just enough extra flour to keep the dough from sticking. Turn dough into a greased bowl and turn the dough over so that it is greased all over. Cover and let rise until doubled in bulk, approximately 1-1/2 hours. When doubled, punch down and let the dough raise for another 3/4 hour. Punch down again and divide the dough into 14 equal parts. Roll these into balls, cover and let rest for 20 minutes.

Now, roll each ball into a flat roll about 1/4 inch thick. Make 5 cuts in each disk, from the edge inward about an inch. Don't cut through to the center. The cuts should be like the spokes in a wheel. Now take the edges of these cuts and fold them into the center, keeping in mind what a Kaiser roll looks like. When all have been folded in, seal the center with a wet finger, punching the dough in. Transfer rolls to a corn meal-dusted, greased cookie sheet, and let rise until doubled in bulk again, about 1 hour. Brush rolls with water and bake in a preheated 425° F oven for 20 minutes, or until browned and done, brushing them with water several more times while baking. Makes 14 rolls.

Refrigerator Rolls

A bowl of nice, yeasty dough in the refrigerator gives me as good a feeling as having several loaves of bread in the freezer. If your family insists on freshly baked bread or rolls at each dinner, this is certainly the recipe for you. Please read Success Tips before beginning.

4 cakes yeast	5 teaspoons salt
1 cup lukewarm water	4 large eggs
1-1/3 cups sugar	12 cups stirred and measured
2 cups lard, margarine, or butter,	white or unbleached white
cut into pieces	flour (part may be whole
3 cups boiling water	wheat flour, in which case use
	part brown sugar)

Dissolve yeast in warm water and let it proof for 5 to 8 minutes. Meanwhile combine the sugar, lard, boiling water, and salt and stir to blend and melt the lard and dissolve the sugar. Cool to lukewarm and then stir in the yeast mixture and beat in the eggs.

Add 6 cups of the flour and beat thoroughly. Then stir in the remaining flour, 1 cup at a time, using only enough to make a medium dough. Turn the dough out onto a lightly floured board and knead lightly. *This dough does not require a great deal of kneading.*

When the dough has been kneaded, place it in a clean, greased bowl and turn the dough so that it has been greased all over. Cover well and place in the refrigerator to be used as desired *over the next week. Remember that the dough will have to be punched down occasionally—several times on the first day, and about once a day thereafter.*

To use, remove the required amount of dough from the refrigerator, and let it rest for 10 minutes. Then roll it out and cut into circles with a biscuit cutter. Place, not too close together, on greased cookie sheets and let rise until doubled, about 45 minutes. Bake in a preheated 375° F oven until golden brown and done, about 25 minutes. If desired the rolls can be placed in greased muffin tins, allowed to rise and baked. This dough also makes good brown-and serve rolls (directions on page 46), and, since it is a sweet, rich dough can be used as the basis for cinnamon rolls.

Recipe makes approximately 8 to 10 dozen rolls.

BUTTERY REFRIGERATOR ROLLS. These are delicious. Great to serve at luncheons. Take the required amount of dough and roll it out on a lightly floured board into a rectangle. Brush with melted butter. Roll up like a jelly roll. With a sharp knife, cut as for jelly rolls. Place each piece, cut side down, in a greased muffin tin. Bake as directed above. Serve hot.

Buttery Scottish Rolls

The flaky deliciousness of these rolls comes from the method of rolling and shaping. Please read Success Tips before beginning.

1 tablespoon or cake of yeast	1 tablespoon sugar
1/2 cup lukewarm water	1 teaspoon salt
2 teaspoons sugar or honey	1 cup lukewarm water
4 cups stirred and measured white	1/2 cup lard
or unbleached white flour	1/2 cup butter or margarine

Combine yeast, 1/2 cup water, and the 2 teaspoons sugar. Let proof for 5 to 8 minutes. While the yeast is proofing combine flour, remaining 1 tablespoon sugar and salt. Beat in the yeast mixture and the remaining 1 cup water. It should form a medium dough. Add a small amount of water, or of flour, if needed. Turn the dough out onto a lightly floured bread board and knead until it is smooth and elastic.

When the dough has been kneaded enough place it in a clean, greased bowl and turn the dough so that it is covered with a thin layer of grease. Cover and let rise until doubled in bulk, about 1-1/2 hours.

When dough has doubled, turn it out onto a lightly floured board and cut into 2 parts. Roll each part into a long rectangle, about 8 inches wide and 16 or 17 inches long. Spread the top third of each rectangle with 1/4 cup softened lard. Fold it over the center, fold the bottom third over the top and turn so that the open end faces you and roll it out again into a rectangle. Now spread the top third with 2 tablespoons of the softened butter, fold it over the center and continue as directed. Roll the dough out and spread with 2 table-spoons butter again, making 3 rollings in all, one with lard and two with butter. After the third rolling, roll the dough out 1/2 inch thick and cut with a floured biscuit cutter. Place on a greased cookie sheet, cover and let rise until almost, but not quite, double in bulk, about 30 to 35 minutes. Bake in a preheated 400° F oven for 20 to 25 minutes or until golden brown and done.

Makes approximately 18 rolls.

Hot Dog Buns

This recipe makes an excellent hot dog bun. It is made according to the RapidMix method of combining the dry ingredients with the yeast. *If you like you might substitute whole wheat flour for half of the white flour, with a little wheat germ for extra nutrition. I sometimes add a package of onion soup mix to the dough, or some finely minced fresh onions.* Please read Success Tips before beginning.

4 to 5 cups stirred and measured white or unbleached white flour	2 teaspoons salt
	1 package dry yeast
	3/4 cup milk
1/4 cup sugar (use brown sugar if using any whole wheat flour)	5 tablespoons butter, margarine, or vegetable oil

In the large bowl of an electric mixer combine 2 cups of the flour with the sugar, salt and dry yeast. Combine the milk and butter and heat until warm. Pour into the dry ingredients, stirring all the while. Beat with the electric mixer at medium speed for 2 minutes, scraping down the sides of the bowl occasionally.

Add another cup of flour, or just enough to make a thick batter. Beat for another 2 minutes, scraping the bowl occasionally.

Now stir in enough additional flour to make a soft dough, turn out onto a lightly floured bread board and knead until smooth and elastic, adding just enough flour to keep from sticking.

Turn dough out into a greased bowl, turning the dough so that it is greased on all sides. Cover and let rise until doubled in bulk. This will take approximately 1 hour.

When dough has doubled, punch it down and divide into 30 pieces. Using the palms of your hands, roll each piece of dough into a rope about 4 or 5 inches long. Place on greased cookie sheets and brush each roll with butter. Cover and let rise for 30 minutes, then bake in a preheated 400° F oven for 20 to 25 minutes or until rolls are browned and done. Makes 30.

Yemenite Potted Bread (Kubaneh)

My children used to call this a "fun bread," especially when I would roll the balls of dough in sesame seeds before placing them in the pot. If you wish you might roll the balls of dough in a strongly flavored garlic butter. The old-fashioned way of baking the dough in a pot seems to go well with winter meals. Please read Success Tips before beginning.

2 cakes yeast	7 to 9 cups stirred and measured
1/2 cup lukewarm water	white or unbleached white
2-1/2 cups lukewarm water	flour
2 teaspoons salt	1/2 to 3/4 cup melted butter or
	margarine

Dissolve yeast in the 1/2 cup water and then stir in the remaining water, salt, and 4 cups of the flour. Beat thoroughly and then add the remaining flour, 1 cup at a time, until the dough is medium firm.

Turn dough out onto a lightly floured surface and knead lightly. Then turn into an oiled bowl and oil the surface of the dough. Cover and let rise until doubled in bulk, about 1 to 1-1/2 hours. When doubled, turn dough out of the pan onto a lightly floured surface again. Cut off pieces of dough and shape into balls. Coat with melted butter and place in a deep pot. I use a cast iron Dutch oven, or a 3-quart Copco pot.

Cover the pot and let dough rise until doubled in bulk again, about 1 hour. Bake uncovered in a preheated 350° F oven for approximately 1 hour, or until done. Turn out of the pot onto a plate and let guests pull off the rolls. These are best served hot.

Orange Sweet Rolls

The potato dough that is used for these rolls can be used for virtually any sweet roll variation that you can think of. The use of leftover mashed potatoes, *unseasoned,* in bread doughs adds moisture and makes a sturdier bread that will stay fresh longer. Please read Success Tips before beginning.

2 cups leftover, unseasoned, mashed potatoes	8 to 9 cups stirred and measured white or unbleached white flour
2 cups milk or half and half	
1 cup butter, margarine, or lard	2 large eggs
1 cup sugar	1 tablespoon vanilla
2 teaspoons salt	3 tablespoons grated fresh orange rind
2 cakes yeast	
1/2 cup lukewarm water	3/4 cup brown sugar

1 tablespoon cinnamon
1/2 to 1 cup chopped walnuts
Orange Glaze (recipe below)

Turn the mashed potatoes into a saucepan and stir in the milk. Add 1/2 cup of the butter, all of the sugar, and the salt. Stir to mix and heat, until the butter melts. Set aside.

Proof the yeast in the 1/2 cup water in a large mixing bowl. Then stir in the potato mixture, 4 cups of the flour, the eggs, vanilla, and 2 tablespoons of the grated orange rind. Beat until smooth and thoroughly mixed. Then add the remaining flour, 1 cup at a time, until it forms a medium dough.

Turn the dough out onto a lightly floured surface and knead just until smooth and elastic, adding just enough flour as needed to make a non-sticky dough. Turn dough into an oiled bowl and rub the surface of the dough with a little oil. Cover and let rise until doubled in bulk, about 1 to 1-1/2 hours. While dough is rising, make the Orange Glaze and prepare the baking pans.

When dough has doubled, punch it down and divide the dough into 2 parts. Roll each portion of dough into a rectangle and brush with 1/2 of the remaining butter, melted. Sprinkle with 1/2 of the brown sugar, cinnamon, remaining grated orange rind, and nuts. Starting with the long side, roll the dough as for a jelly roll. Cut each roll of dough into 12 even pieces and place these, cut side down, over the Orange Glaze, in buttered 9- by 13- by 2-inch pans. Brush the tops of the rolls with a little more melted butter, cover and let rise until almost, but not quite doubled in bulk, about 30 to 40 minutes.

Bake the rolls in a preheated 350° F oven for 30 minutes, or until browned and done. Yield is 24 rolls. Serve warm. These rolls freeze very well.

ORANGE GLAZE. In a small saucepan, combine 1 cup sugar, 2/3 cup fresh orange juice, 1/2 cup butter or margarine, and 2 tablespoons grated fresh orange rind. Cook, stirring, over medium heat until syrupy, about 8 to 10 minutes. Pour half the glaze into each of two 9- by 13- by 2-inch pans and place the rolls over the glaze.

Apple Sweet Rolls

These are rich and delicious. Please read Success Tips before beginning.

Dough

1/2 cup skim milk crystals dissolved in 1 cup water	2 cakes yeast dissolved in 2/3 cup lukewarm water
3 tablespoons sugar	7 to 9 cups stirred and measured
3 tablespoons vegetable oil	white or unbleached white
3/4 teaspoon salt	flour

Filling

1 can apple pie filling	1 cup raisins
1 cup brown or granulated white sugar	chopped nuts (optional) cinnamon (optional)

Combine reconstituted milk crystals with sugar, oil and salt. Add the dissolved yeast and 4 cups of the flour. Beat until it forms a smooth batter. Then begin adding the remaining flour one cup at a time until it forms a smooth, medium firm dough. Turn the dough out onto a lightly floured bread board and knead until it is smooth and elastic.

Turn dough into a clean, greased bowl and turn the dough so that it is lightly greased on all sides. Cover and let rise until doubled. This will take approximately 1 to 1-1/2 hours. Repeat once.

When the dough has doubled in bulk, punch it down and turn it out onto a lightly floured bread board. Roll the dough out into a large rectangle. Brush the dough very lightly with melted butter or margarine, or with a light vegetable oil. Spread the dough with half of the sugar, all of the apple pie filling and then cover with the remaining sugar, the raisins and some chopped nuts if desired. Sprinkle with some cinnamon. Roll the dough up the long way, patching any hole that might form.

Using a very sharp knife, cut the roll into 1-1/4-inch slices. Place the rolls, cut side down, in a large greased baking pan with sides. Cover and let rise again until just doubled.

When rolls are doubled, bake them in a preheated 375° F oven for 15 to 18 minutes or until browned and done. Remove to racks and brush lightly with melted butter or margarine and cool. Frost when cool. Makes 15.

Frosting

2 cups powdered sugar	4 ounces cream cheese
1/4 cup butter or margarine	1 teaspoon vanilla extract

Blend thoroughly until mixture is heavy. Spread, or pour, over the rolls.

Hungarian Nut Rolls

As is typical of Hungarian pastries, the dough is rich with egg yolks. Be sure to separate the eggs when cold, but let the yolks warm to room temperature before using. I pour the whites into a small container, mark how many whites there are and freeze them. When there are enough I make an Angel Food Cake, or a spectacular meringue dessert. Please read Success Tips before beginning.

7 large egg yolks	1 cake yeast
1/2 teaspoon salt	3 to 4 cups stirred and measured
1 cup milk or half and half that has	white or unbleached white
been scalded and cooled	flour

Filling

1 cup minus 2 tablespoons butter	1 cup ground walnuts or almonds
or margarine, softened	1/4 cup cream or half and half
1 cup finely granulated sugar	1 tablespoon sugar

Combine egg yolks, salt, milk and yeast. Make certain before adding the yeast that the mixture is lukewarm and not cold. Stir to mix and then beat in 2 cups of the flour. Beat thoroughly and then add another cup of flour and just enough more to make a dough that is soft to medium and not sticky. Turn the dough out onto a lightly floured surface and knead gently. Then turn into a greased bowl and turn the dough so that it is greased all over, cover and let rise for 45 minutes.

While the dough is rising make the filling. Cream the softened butter with the sugar until it's light. Add the ground (or finely chopped) nuts. Set aside.

After the dough has risen, punch it down and cut in half. Turn 1 portion of the dough onto a *very* lightly floured surface and roll with a lightly floured rolling pin into a thin rectangle. This dough can be rolled very thin. Spread with 1/2 of the filling and roll the dough up, jelly-roll style. Cut into 1/2-inch slices and place on a greased jelly-roll pan. *The pan used should have sides as the filling will leak.* Press the roll down a little with your fingers, and continue until all of the rolls are made. Cover and let rise for 30 minutes.

Bake in a preheated 375° F oven for 20 to 25 minutes, or until golden brown and done. Halfway through the baking time, brush the rolls with a mixture of the 1/4 cup cream and the sugar. When rolls are done cool them on a rack. If you wish you might brush them with a thin powdered sugar glaze; however, these rolls are so rich that it isn't really necessary. Makes 2 to 3 dozen rolls.

MID-EASTERN NUT ROLLS. You can give these rolls a definite Mid-Eastern touch by using almonds and adding a tablespoon — or more if desired — of rose water or orange-flower to the filling. Add another teaspoon of the same to the cream and sugar.

Butter Dips

This recipe was developed about ten years ago, by one of the flour companies in their eternal search for new ways in which to use flour. It's good, and I like to add some minced, or powdered, garlic to the melted butter, and maybe some grated Parmesan or Romano cheese. Just be careful not to overmix the dough.

1/2 cup butter or margarine	1 tablespoon sugar
2 cups stirred and measured white or unbleached white flour	1 tablespoon baking powder
	2 large eggs
1 teaspoon salt	1/2 cup milk

Put the butter in a 9- by 13- by 2-inch baking pan and place in a 450° F oven until melted.

Combine the dry ingredients and stir until thoroughly mixed. Beat the eggs and milk together and stir, all at once, into the dry ingredients. Turn the dough out onto a lightly floured bread board and knead no more than 10 times, just until the dough holds together. Then pat the dough out, using your hands, until it is about 1/2 inch thick. Cut into oblong shapes. Place in the pan and turn the dips over so that each side is coated with butter. Bake at 450° F until browned and done, about 15 minutes. Makes approximately 12.

Crumpets

Similar to an English muffin, the crumpet is soggier and has more holes in it. Crumpets are delicious toasted and laden with butter and a nice homemade jam. They also freeze well. If you don't have the small muffin rings, use 7-ounce tuna cans that have had both top and bottom neatly removed. Please read Success tips before you begin.

2 cups scalded milk
1/2 cup butter or margarine
1 cake yeast
1 teaspoon sugar
1/2 cup lukewarm water

3 to 4 cups stirred and measured white or unbleached white flour
3/4 teaspoon baking soda
1 tablespoon hot water

Pour scalded milk over the butter and stir to melt the butter. Cool to lukewarm. Dissolve the yeast and sugar in 1/2 cup lukewarm water and let proof for 5 minutes. Add to milk mixture and beat in 2 cups of the flour. Beat thoroughly and then add just enough of the remaining flour to make a heavy batter. Cover and let rise until batter is light and bubbly.

Mix baking soda with the hot water and stir into batter. Beat thoroughly, cover and let rise again. Pour, no more than 1/3 to 1/2 inch deep, into buttered rings on a moderately hot buttered griddle. Cook until crumpets are dry and the bubbles have broken through the tops. Remove rings, turn and brown lightly on the other side. Split and serve hot, or toasted. Makes approximately 12.

Quick And Easy Muffins

Just heat the oven. These are the quickest and lightest muffins ever.

2 cups stirred and measured self-rising flour (see page 38)
1 cup milk
1/4 cup mayonnaise, homemade preferred

Combine ingredients and mix well, but not too much. Pour into greased muffin tins and bake in a preheated 400° F oven for 12 minutes, or until browned and done. Makes approximately 10 to 12 medium muffins.

Best Fruit Muffins

These delicious fruit muffins can be made with canned or cooked fruit, fresh berries, or cut-up, well-drained fresh fruit. If you want a marvelous plain muffin, simply omit the fruit and substitute milk for the fruit juice.

2-1/2 cups stirred and measured white or unbleached white flour	2 large eggs
	1/2 cup vegetable oil
	1/2 cup fruit juice or milk
1/3 cup sugar	1 teaspoon vanilla
1 tablespoon baking powder	1 cup cut up fresh fruit, well
1/2 teaspoon salt	drained, or drained canned or cooked fruit

Stir together the flour, sugar, baking powder and salt. Beat the eggs with the oil, fruit juice, and vanilla. Add liquid mixture to dry ingredients and stir just until thoroughly moistened. *Do not over-mix.* Spoon into well-greased muffin tins and bake in a preheated 350° F oven for 20 minutes, or until done. Makes 14 muffins.

Peanut Butter and Jelly Muffins

No matter how delicious the meal I prepare, to my small grandsons there is nothing that beats peanut butter and jelly. Naturally, this is their favorite muffin.

2 cups stirred and measured white or unbleached white flour	1/2 teaspoon salt
	3/4 cup crunchy peanut butter
1/2 cup sugar	3/4 cup milk
1 tablespoon baking powder	2 large eggs
1/3 cup jam, preserves, or jelly	

Combine the dry ingredients and stir together. Cut in the peanut butter as you would butter, until the mixture resembles a very coarse meal. Add the milk and the eggs, all at once, stirring until the dry mixture is well moistened. Spoon 2 tablespoons of batter into each of

18 well-greased muffin tins. Drop a teaspoon of jam in the center of each and top with 2 more tablespoons of batter. Bake in a preheated 400° F oven for 15 to 20 minutes, or until done.

Note. To increase the nutritional value, use 1/4 cup wheat germ in place of as much flour. To increase it still further, this is a perfect recipe for using the Cornell Triple-Rich Formula (page 43). That way the children can have their sweet, and still be nourished by it.

Cheese Biscuits

These are an excellent cheese-flavored addition to any breakfast or brunch. I make the biscuits in quantity and freeze them. It's a real timesaver. With all biscuits, be careful not to overmix the dough.

6 cups stirred and measured white or unbleached flour	1-1/2 teaspoons cream of tartar
3 tablespoons baking powder	1-1/2 cups butter, margarine or shortening
2 tablespoons sugar	1 pound medium or sharp cheese, grated
2 teaspoons salt	
2 cups milk, approximately	

Stir the dry ingredients together so that they are thoroughly mixed. Cut the butter in until the mixture is like small peas. Add the cheese and then just enough milk to make a dough that can be worked. Turn out onto a lightly floured surface and work the dough *just barely enough so that it holds together. This is the secret of good biscuits. You do not actually knead them.* Now *pat* the dough out to a thickness of approximately 1/2 inch. Cut with a floured cutter or glass. Bake immediately on lightly greased cookie sheets in a preheated 425° F oven until browned and done, approximately 12 to 15 minutes.

If you wish to freeze the biscuits, freeze them *before* baking. They will actually be better. Simply place biscuits on a cookie sheet and freeze until solid. Then place in freezer bags until ready to bake. Bake at 325° F for 10 minutes and then at 450° F for another 10 minutes, or until browned and done. Makes 5 to 6 dozen.

Cream Biscuits

In these delicious biscuits the heavy cream provides both fat and liquid. The key to making biscuits that are light and flaky is in the mixing. Biscuits must be mixed *very lightly,* and then *patted* out on a very lightly floured surface *with your hands*. Forget the rolling pin when making biscuits. For a sweet biscuit for the children, you might want to sprinkle these with maple or brown sugar, before baking.

2 cups stirred and measured unbleached white or white flour	1 tablespoon baking powder 1 teaspoon salt 1 cup heavy cream, whipped

Combine dry ingredients and stir together. Stir in the cream, mixing it in lightly with a fork. You might need a little more cream. Turn dough out on a floured board and knead no more than 10 times. Pat the dough to a thickness of 1/2 inch and cut with a floured cutter. Bake in a preheated 450° F oven for 10 to 12 minutes, or until golden brown and done.

Makes 10 to 12 biscuits, depending on size.

Orange Biscuits

We don't very often think of the lowly biscuit as being glamorous. However, with just a few additions the biscuit can be made into a glamorous addition to any brunch or luncheon. I've used a combination of orange liqueur and orange-flower water here, but you could use all orange liqueur, or even orange juice if you must.

2 cups stirred and measured white or unbleached white flour 1 tablespoon baking powder 1/2 to 1 teaspoon salt 3 or 4 tablespoons cold margarine, butter or lard	1 tablespoon grated orange rind 1/2 cup rich milk 1/4 cup orange curacao, or Triple Sec 12 to 15 cubes of sugar 1/4 cup orange-flower water
powdered sugar	

Sift dry ingredients together and cut in the margarine until it is the size of small peas. Do not overmix. Add the orange rind and milk and then the liqueur. Stir quickly and knead very lightly, just until all ingredients are moistened. Pat the dough out until it is about 1/3 inch thick and cut into twice as many rounds as you want biscuits.

Place half of the rounds on a greased cookie sheet. Top each with a cube of sugar moistened with the orange-flower water. Cover with another round. Bake in a preheated 450° F oven until browned and done, about 15 minutes. Spread tops with some powdered sugar moistened with more orange liqueur. Serve hot. Makes 12 to 15 biscuits.

Cheese Snack Biscuits

I enjoy serving these with *quiche* and salad and a dry wine. If desired, these can be cut and placed close together on a cookie sheet. Freeze solid and then place in freezer bags. Bake, still frozen, as directed below for 15 to 18 minutes, or until browned and done.

1 pound Cheddar cheese, grated
1/2 cup butter or margarine
1/2 cup cool water

1-1/2 cups stirred and measured
    white or unbleached white
    flour
1/2 teaspoon salt
1/2 teaspoon baking powder

Seasonings

1 package onion soup mix
or a mixture of 1/4 teaspoon:
    each cayenne and paprika

or a mixture of 1 tablespoon
    Worcestershire sauce and
    1/2 teaspoon cayenne

Cream the cheese and butter. Add water and then the dry ingredients which have been stirred together thoroughly. If dough is firm enough, form it into a roll, wrap in waxed paper and chill for several hours. If it isn't firm enough, simply chill the dough in the bowl, or else add barely enough flour to make a dough that will roll.

When dough is thoroughly chilled either cut it into thin slices, or else roll the dough out on a lightly floured bread board and cut into thin shapes. Place biscuits on greased cookie sheet and bake in a preheated 450° F oven for 7 to 10 minutes, or until golden brown and done. Makes 2 to 3 dozen depending on how thin the dough is rolled and cut.

Sourdough Breads

SOURDOUGH has been around for as long as man has been eating leavened bread, because for the thousands of years that leavened bread has been baked by man, a piece of dough from one batch has often been saved to leaven the next. This method began; perhaps, when some early cook neglected a simple flour and water dough which then trapped some airborne wild yeasts, fermented, and became light. Perhaps the light dough was baked by itself in hot ashes or on hot stones, and was discovered to taste good. Or perhaps it was added to another batch of flour and water and the subsequent leavened bread, when baked, was discovered to have an appealing lightness and zesty flavor.

In more recent times, sourdough has belonged to the far west and to old prospectors, mountain men, sheepherders, and miners, who were dependent upon their pail of sourdough to provide them with a daily ration of breads and biscuits. Sourdough was an integral part of life in the old west, where there was no refrigeration and distances between trading posts were great. It was the only practical leaven, and the pot of sourdough starter was a cherished item in any household. Some starters were kept for so many years that they were passed from generation to generation, and were part of a daughter's dowry. And it is true that the older a starter is the better it is, as long as it is active and has been replenished regularly.

Except with the lone men of the west, sourdough fell out of favor when commercial yeast was developed and became popular. Yeast was easier to work with and to keep than was sourdough, which required feeding and care. Our bread-eating nation gradually progressed, or regressed, to the soft, cottony loaves of flour-filled air that until recently were generally considered acceptable bread. But in the past decade there has been a resurgence of interest in bread as a "staff of life" rather than as a meal filler or a soggy recipient of sandwich ingredients. And with this renewed interest in bread, there has been a sudden and enormous interest in sourdough—an interest which, so far, has not abated.

Sourdough fanciers seem to be divided between those who use yeast with the sourdough, and those who claim that if the recipe uses yeast, "it just ain't sourdough." I disagree with the latter. I realize that a bread using yeast as well as sourdough won't have quite as strong a sourdough flavor as will a strictly sourdough bread, but as far as I'm concerned, if a recipe uses sourdough starter as an ingredient it's a sourdough recipe, whether or not it also calls for yeast. And I happen to enjoy the security of using yeast. Most of the time I use it along with the sourdough, although occasionally I don't.

Sourdough has become a passion with many people, and I've been fortunate enough to meet some of them. One of my favorite "sourdough couples" is Chuck and Mary Dunham of Pocatello, Idaho. This exuberant couple began their honeymoon fourteen years ago with a bread-baking contest, and have continued their competition ever since. And sourdough has become such a shared passion with this couple that it is almost an obsession. They both consider the pursuit of sourdough to be the most exciting food adventure you can have, because you can be as creative as you wish with it. They have been creative, and have also been very willing to share the results of their experiments.

Mary Dunham proofs all of her bread, sourdough and otherwise, in the microwave oven, using the lowest setting. She covers the bread dough with plastic wrap or waxed paper, and sets the pan of dough in the oven, turning the pan every 5 minutes until the dough is almost doubled. The total process takes no more than 20 minutes, although she does make it clear that proofing time depends not only on the total volume, but also on its distribution. This means simply that a shallow wide pan of bread dough will rise faster than a deep narrow pan of dough.

The Dunhams have been using the same starter for over 15 years, adding to it as needed. When the starter bubbles over the tops and sides of the container, Chuck scrapes the dried starter off the sides of the container, puts this into a small bowl, and places the bowl in a warm spot to allow the sourdough to dry thoroughly. Once dried, this instant starter makes a nice gift to other enthusiasts. All you have to do is add it to a mixture of equal parts flour and tepid water that have been blended smooth, and give it 48 hours to proof before you use it.

I have experimented with all kinds of starters, and with all kinds of liquids used in making those starters. The Milk Starter is still my favorite, although the Yogurt Starter is a close second. In any starter that uses water as the liquid ingredient, you can substitute beer with excellent results. Many readers of my earlier books and of my local recipe column have told me of using rice, potato, or macaroni water as the liquid with excellent results.

Converting Regular Recipes to Sourdough

Virtually any bread recipe can be converted to sourdough. It's a simple matter of controlling the leavening action and the moisture content. One home economist I know recommends the following method. For each 1- or 2-loaf recipe, omit 1-3/4 cups liquid, add 2 cups starter, and cut back on the flour by 1/2 to 1 cup.

I think that my way is even simpler. Since you always add flour to make a dough of a medium or medium-firm consistency, I simply don't worry about exact amounts For each 1- or 2-loaf recipe, I cut the yeast to 1 cake and add 1 cup of starter. It's as simple as that.

Success Tips for Sourdough

1.   Never store sourdough starter in a metal container. Don't even mix it in a metal container. Use crockery, glass or plastic.

2.   Keep the starter refrigerated. If you are not planning on using it for a long period of time, freeze the starter. This can safely be done several times without harming the starter. Just remember to

allow the starter to come to room temperature gradually, and do not try to thaw it by heating it over direct heat. When properly cared for, the starter will keep indefinitely.

3. Make certain that the starter is at room temperature each time you use it. And when you replenish the starter, let it stand at room temperature until it bubbles before refrigerating.

4. If you do not use the starter at least once every 10 days, freshen it by pouring off half of the starter and adding an equal amount of liquid and flour. Let it stand until it is good and bubbly, and then refrigerate.

5. It's a good idea to clean the sourdough container thoroughly when you replenish the starter, or every week to 10 days. I simply pour off the starter into a mixing bowl, and pop the container into the dishwasher for a good scouring.

6. The liquid that rises to the top of the starter is harmless -- just stir it back in. I've always been told that if the starter turns green to throw it out, but to go ahead and fix it up and use it if it turns orange. I've never had one turn green, but if I did I *would* throw it out. However, if one begins to turn orange, simply pour some of it off and discard. Then replenish the remainder as usual and leave it out for a day. It should be as good as new.

7. As mentioned in the foreword to the chapter, a variety of liquids can be used in the starters. The most important thing is to be consistent. If you began the starter with milk, then each time you replenish it use milk. The same goes for beer or for water.

8. If you're fond of a particular kind of flour — say that you *always* use whole wheat flour — then make the starter using that kind of flour. Whole wheat flour is always a good choice and the starter can be used in other whole-grain breads with great success.

9. A good starter can be made with white flour, unbleached white, rye or whole wheat flours. Never use self-rising flour. I see no reason why buckwheat or potato flour couldn't be used. However, I have not experimented with them and so cannot speak from personal experience.

10. Most oldtime cooks deplore, sometimes quite loudly, the use of yeast in sourdough recipes, and if you have a good, active starter you can safely omit the yeast when it is called for. By the same token, if a recipe doesn't call for yeast, it is always safe to add a cake or two. If you add yeast, dissolve the cake in a 1/4 cup of water before using. You

will probably need a small amount of extra flour, but this is easily added during the mixing.

11.   A lot of sourdough recipes call for the addition of a teaspoon of baking soda or baking powder. I've never found this to be necessary. When I use a recipe from a friend who always adds the soda or baking powder, I leave it in. But it can be omitted. And if you do insist on using one or the other, remember that in sourdough recipes, at least, they are interchangeable.

My Favorite Starter

1 or 2 cups milk   equal amount of flour

Put the milk in a sterilized glass or pottery container, cover with cheesecloth, and let stand at room temperature for 24 hours. Then stir in an equal amount of flour and blend well. Cover with cheesecloth and set the jar outdoors in a protected place for 12 to 24 hours. Now put the jar in a warm place — the back of the stove will be fine — until it becomes full of bubbles. This will take from 2 to 5 days, depending on the weather and on the wild yeast cells in the air. Put the starter in a covered container, being careful to leave room enough in the container for the starter to rise a bit without bubbling over. Store in the refrigerator. Each time the starter is used, allow it to come to room temperature before using and to remain at room temperature after replenishing, until it bubbles.

Old Time Sourdough Starter

This is a good starter, and better, to my mind, than some of the other "quick" starters. The vinegar gives it a good, clean odor and sour flavor. Remember to read Success Tips before starting.

2 cups stirred and measured flour   1 tablespoon salt
2 tablespoons sugar   1-1/2 cups lukewarm water
              1 tablespoon vinegar

Combine ingredients thoroughly. The mixture will be thick. Cover and let sit for at least 24 hours before using. When you use the starter, replenish it each time by adding an equal quantity of warm water and flour and a teaspoon of sugar. Cover with a cloth again and let it stand for several hours, or overnight, until it is full of bubbles again.

Reed Hansen's Sourdough Starter

Reed Hansen is a colorful Idaho Falls farmer, vice-chairman of the State Water Resources Board, and avid sourdough buff who does all of the bread baking in his home. An enthusiastically creative cook, he loves to experiment and once got so carried away with his enthusiasm for a recipe that he ended up with 200 doughnuts. He's been more careful since then. This is his favorite starter. Please read Success Tips before beginning.

2 cups stirred and measured flour	1 to 4 tablespoons sugar
1 teaspoon salt	2 cups potato, rice or macaroni water

Combine all ingredients in a crockery or glass container. Cover with a cloth or a loose lid (do not seal). Let stand in a warm place for about 5 days. It will bubble and smell, but the more pungent the odor the better the starter.

   Note. You can add a cake of yeast to this starter to speed up the process to only 3 days.

Yogurt Sourdough Starter

This recipe is a fairly recent development in the sourdough saga, and results in a marvelously tangy, zesty sourdough starter, especially good if you like a lively sourdough flavor rather than a bland one. It has replaced the milk-flour starter as my particular favorite. Use skim milk, and low fat yogurt for a more zesty sourdough, and whole milk and a plain, unflavored yogurt for a more bland sourdough. Please read Success Tips before beginning.

1 cup skim, low-fat or whole milk (see above) heated to barely lukewarm	2 tablespoons plain or low fat yogurt (see above)
	1 cup stirred and measured flour

Combine the milk and yogurt and turn into a warm bowl. Cover and let stand in a warm place for 18 to 24 hours. The temperature should not be too warm. Above 110 degrees will kill the bacteria, but don't let it go below 70 degrees either. After 18 to 24 hours, the starter will be just like homemade yogurt, which is exactly what it is at this point. If the starter has begun to set properly, a curd will have formed. If there is a clear liquid at the top, simply stir it back into the mixture. However, if the liquid or the starter have turned pinkish, discard what you have and begin again.

Stir the flour into the mixture until it is smooth. Cover and let stand in a warm place until it is full of bubbles and has a good zesty, sour smell. This will take from 2 to 5 days. At the end of that time refrigerate the starter, or use it. Allow the starter to come to room temperature before using.

To replenish after using, stir in equal parts of lukewarm milk and flour, cover and allow to stand in a warm place for several hours or overnight until it is full of bubbles again. Then cover and store in the refrigerator until needed. Remember always to be consistent in the type of milk used. Don't use skim milk one time and whole milk another time.

Basic Sourdough Bread

This makes a good, basic sourdough bread with a good flavor. You can substitute white flour for whole wheat flour without any other changes. Be sure to read Success Tips before starting.

1 cup sourdough starter	1/2 cup skim milk crystals
1 cup lukewarm water	2 tablespoons honey, brown sugar,
1 tablespoon vinegar	or other sweetener
1 cup stirred and measured white	1/4 cup salad oil, melted butter, or
or whole wheat flour	other shortening
1/4 cup lukewarm water	2 teaspoons salt
2 cakes yeast	5-1/2 to 6-1/2 cups stirred and
1 cup lukewarm water	measured white or whole
	wheat flour

In a large mixing bowl combine the starter, 1 cup water, vinegar and 1 cup flour. Mix until smooth, cover and let set in a warm place overnight. In the morning stir the starter down and add the 1/4 cup water in which the yeast has been dissolved. Then add the 1 cup water, the skim milk crystals, sweetening, oil and salt. Stir all together and then add 2 cups of the flour and stir until smooth.

Add the remaining flour a cup at a time, stirring each cup in until the mixture is smooth. Use only enough flour to make a medium dough. Turn the dough out onto a lightly floured bread board and knead until it is smooth and elastic. Now turn the dough into a lightly oiled bowl, turn the dough around so that it has a light film of oil all over, cover the bowl and let the dough rise until doubled. This will take approximately 1 hour for this recipe because of the added yeast.

When dough has risen, turn it out onto a very lightly floured bread board, punch it down, knead it some more and then cut and shape. This amount of dough will make two 8-by 4-by 2-inch loaves, or 18 to 24 dinner rolls depending on the size. However you shape the dough, let it rise until doubled if you have used white flour, and until almost, but not quite doubled, if you have used whole wheat flour. Bake in a 375° F oven for 40 to 45 minutes for the loaves, and for 20 to 25 minutes for the rolls.

Sourdough Sandwich Bread

This makes a delicious sandwich bread with a mild sourdough flavor and increased flavor from the chicken broth. The shredded wheat adds a crunchy texture that is delightful in sandwiches.

1 cup sourdough starter
1 tablespoon molasses, brown sugar, or honey
1-1/2 cups chicken broth
1 cup lukewarm water
4-1/2 cups white flour, stirred and measured
1 tablespoon salt
1/4 cup salad oil, melted butter, or margarine
3 cups whole wheat flour, stirred and measured
1-1/2 cups crushed shredded wheat biscuits

The night before you plan on baking the bread, mix the sourdough with the molasses, chicken broth, water and 3 cups of the white flour. Stir to mix thoroughly, cover and let sit in a warm place overnight. In the morning add the salt and the oil and stir to mix. Now begin adding the remaining white flour and the whole wheat flour, 1 cup at a time, using just enough to make a soft dough. Then knead in the crushed shredded wheat. Turn out onto a lightly floured bread board, using either any unused whole wheat flour, or some white flour, and knead lightly. The dough will be sticky. Cut in half and place each part in a buttered standard 9-inch bread pan. Cover with a clean cloth and let rise until dough is even with the tops of the pans. Bake in a 375°F oven for 50 minutes, or until loaves are browned and test done. Remove from pans and cool on racks.

Reed Hansen's Sourdough Bread

Hansen has won several blue ribbons at the Eastern Idaho State Fair with this bread. Please read Success Tips before beginning.

Reed Hansen's Sourdough Starter (see page 103)	2 cups water 2 cups flour
1 quart sourdough from above mixture	3/4 to 1 cup sugar
1 quart lukewarm water (use potato, rice or macaroni water if possible)	1 tablespoon salt 1/3 cup salad oil, melted butter, or margarine 12 cups flour, stirred and measured

Begin the night before by mixing the starter with the 2 cups each of water and flour. Mix well, cover and let sit in a warm place overnight.

In the morning take a quart of sourdough from the mixture. Pour the remaining sourdough into your starter crock and refrigerate it. Mix the quart of starter with the water, sugar, salt and oil. Add enough flour to make a medium soft, but not sticky dough. Knead well, until it is smooth and elastic. Rub the dough all over with oil, place in a clean bowl, cover and let rise until doubled.

When the dough has doubled, punch it down and let it rise again. After this second rising, punch the dough down, knead it lightly, and cut it into 4 pieces. Shape each piece into a loaf, and place each in a buttered standard 9-inch bread pan. Cover and let rise again. Bake the loaves in a preheated 350° F oven for 35 to 45 minutes, or until the loaves are browned and done.

Sourdough Granola Bread

This is a delicious, heavy, filling bread. You can use any of the various kinds of granola in it, including homemade. I use no sugar other than what is in the granola. However, if you wish a sweeter bread you can add 1/3 to 1/2 cup of brown sugar. Please read Success Tips before beginning.

1 cake yeast
3/4 cup lukewarm water
2 cups sourdough starter
1 tablespoon salt
3 large eggs, slightly beaten

2 cups granola
2 cups stirred and measured white
flour
2 cups stirred and measured whole
wheat flour

Combine yeast and water and let proof for 5 to 8 minutes. Then stir in the starter, salt, eggs, granola, and the first 2 cups of flour. Mix together thoroughly and add the whole wheat flour, 1 cup at a time, using only enough to make a medium dough. It will still be sticky.

Turn the dough out onto a lightly floured bread board and knead for 4 to 5 minutes. Then rub the dough all over with a tiny amount of oil and place in a buttered 8-inch bread pan. Cover and let rise until doubled, approximately 1-1/2 to 2 hours. When dough has doubled, bake it in a preheated 375°F oven for 35 to 40 minutes, or until browned and done. Turn out of pan onto rack to cool. Makes 1 loaf.

Sourdough Whole Wheat Bread

This makes a delicious bread, and is especially good — as are all whole wheat breads — when made with freshly ground whole wheat flour. There's a noticeable difference that must be tasted to be believed. Be sure to read Success Tips before beginning.

3 cups lukewarm water
1 cup skim milk crystals
2 cakes yeast
6 cups whole wheat flour, stirred
and measured

3 to 4 cups white flour, stirred and
and measured
1-1/4 cups sourdough starter
1/3 cup molasses, brown sugar, or
honey

5 teaspoons salt
1/4 cup salad oil, melted butter,
or margarine

In a large bowl combine the water, skim milk crystals, and yeast. Stir and let it stand for 5 to 8 minutes or until the yeast is foamy. Now stir in the 6 cups of whole wheat flour and the starter. Stir vigorously until mixture is smooth. Then cover and let the sponge stand until it is light and foamy, approximately 1 to 2 hours depending on the warmth of the room.

Stir down the sponge and stir in the molasses, salt, and salad oil. Gradually add the white flour, 1 cup at a time, until you have a medium stiff dough. Turn this dough out onto a very lightly floured board and knead until smooth and elastic. Rub the ball of dough all over with oil and place in a clean bowl, cover and let rise again until doubled, about 1 to 1-1/2 hours.

When the dough has doubled, punch it down and knead it very lightly again. Divide into 2 parts and shape each part into a loaf. Place in buttered standard 9-inch bread pans, cover and let rise until the dough has proofed about 3/4 of its volume, in other words, not quite double. Bake in a preheated 375° F oven for 35 to 45 minutes, or until nicely browned and done. Cool on racks. Makes 2 loaves.

Sourdough Whole Wheat Cheese Bread

This is an absolutely delicious bread, and makes great sandwiches. I frequently bake this in the long baquette pans, and cut the baked loaves in the middle so that I can get four "Poor Boy" type sandwiches out of the two loaves. If you don't like the wheat or graham flour, you can use all unbleached white flour without making any other changes. Please read Success Tips before beginning.

1-1/2 cups sourdough starter
1/2 cup dry milk crystals
   mixed with 1-1/4 cups
   lukewarm water
2 tablespoons sugar
2 teaspoons salt
1 large egg, slightly beaten

3 tablespoons salad oil or melted
   butter or margarine
2 cups grated Cheddar cheese
1/2 cup minced onion that has
   been sautéed until soft
5 to 6 cups stirred and measured
   flour, half of it whole
   wheat or graham flour

Add the reconstituted milk, sugar, and salt to the sourdough starter and mix well. Add the egg, salad oil, cheese and onion and stir together. Stir in the flour 1 cup at a time, using just the amount needed to make a medium dough. Turn the dough out onto a floured bread board and knead until smooth and elastic. Shape into loaves and place directly into buttered 9-inch loaf pans without letting the dough rise first. Then cover and set in a warm place to rise until doubled, approximately 2 to 3 hours. Bake in a preheated 375° F oven for 30 to 45 minutes, or until bread tests done. If it browns too soon, cover with a tent of aluminum foil. Makes 2 loaves.

SOURDOUGH BACON CHEESE BREAD. Cook 6 to 8 slices of bacon until crisp. Drain and crumble. Add to the dough along with the cheese and onion.

Three Cheeses Sourdough Bread

This bread is not only delicious, but it is good for you. Combining cheeses makes a better bread than using only one cheese, and of course a bread like this makes great sandwiches. Please read Success Tips before beginning.

2 cakes yeast	2 tablespoons salad oil, melted
2 cups lukewarm water	butter, or margarine
1 cup sourdough starter	1 tablespoon sugar
1-1/2 cups creamed cottage cheese	2 tablespoons salt
1-1/4 cups grated mild or sharp	6-1/2 to 7-1/2 cups stirred and
Cheddar cheese	measured white or
1-1/4 cups grated Swiss cheese	unbleached white
2 or 3 tablespoons sesame seeds	flour

Dissolve the yeast in the water and set aside to proof for 5 or 8 minutes. Meanwhile measure the starter into a large mixing bowl. Add the cheeses, sesame seed, salad oil, sugar and salt. Stir together and then add the yeast mixture.

Add the flour gradually, 1 cup at a time, until you have a medium-stiff dough. Turn the dough out onto a very lightly floured board and knead thoroughly. When dough has been kneaded, rub it all over with oil and place in a clean bowl. Cover and let rise until doubled in bulk, approximately 45 minutes to an hour.

When dough has doubled, punch it down and shape into 2 loaves. Place loaves in greased 9-inch bread pans and cover and let rise again until doubled, approximately 45 minutes to an hour. Bake in a preheated 375°F oven for 40 to 45 minutes, or until bread is browned and tests done.

Makes 2 loaves.

Buckwheat Sourdough Bread

This makes a good, heavy bread that is excellent toasted, and makes good sandwiches. Please read Success Tips before beginning.

2 cups sourdough starter
1/2 cup lukewarm water
1 teaspoon sugar
1 cake yeast
1 cup lukewarm water mixed with
   1/4 to 1/3 cup dry milk
   crystals
1/4 cup brown sugar or molasses

3 cups stirred and measured
   buckwheat flour
1/4 cup salad oil, melted butter, or
   margarine
1-1/2 teaspoons salt
3 to 4 cups stirred and measured
   white flour

Pour the sourdough starter into a large mixing bowl. Combine the 1/2 cup water, sugar, and yeast and set aside until foamy, about 5 to 8 minutes. Then add to the starter along with the reconstituted milk, brown sugar, buckwheat flour, salad oil and salt. Stir together thoroughly. Then add the white flour 1 cup at a time, mixing each cup in thoroughly. You will need a total of 6 to 7 cups flour. Save at least 1/2 cup to spread on the bread board. Use only enough flour to make a medium-firm dough.

Turn the dough out onto the floured bread board and knead until the mass of dough is smooth, nonsticky and elastic. Rub the dough all over with oil, turn into a clean bowl, cover with a towel and let rise until doubled.

When the dough has doubled, punch it down and turn out onto a very lightly floured bread board again. Cut into pieces and shape as desired. This amount of dough will make 2 smaller loaves, or 1 large loaf. Whatever pans you use, butter them generously. Turn the shaped loaves into the pans, cover and let rise again until not quite doubled. Bake in a preheated 375° F oven for 30 to 45 minutes, depending on the size of the loaves. Five minutes before the bread is done brush the tops of the loaves with cream or evaporated milk.

Sourdough Onion Lovers' Twisted Bread

This bread is as impressive to look at as to eat. And it smells great, too. When I've been in too much of a hurry to braid the dough properly, I've just rolled the dough out, spread it with the filling and then rolled it up jelly-roll style and baked it in a regular loaf pan. Please read Success Tips before beginning.

1 cake yeast
1/4 cup lukewarm water
1 cup sourdough starter
1/2 cup salad oil, melted butter,
  or margarine
1/2 cup regular or reconstituted
  milk

1/2 cup lukewarm water
2 tablespoons honey or sugar
1-1/2 teaspoons salt
1 large egg, beaten
4 to 5 cups stirred and measured
  white flour

Filling

1/4 cup salad oil, melted
  butter or margarine
1 cup finely minced onion
2 large cloves of garlic, minced

1/4 cup grated Parmesan or other
  hard cheese
1 tablespoon sesame or poppy
  seeds

1 teaspoon paprika

To make the dough, dissolve the yeast in the 1/4 cup lukewarm water. Let stand until foamy, approximately 5 to 8 minutes. Then stir in the sourdough starter, salad oil, milk, warm water, sugar, salt and the beaten egg. Then add 2 cups of the flour and mix thoroughly. Add the remaining flour 1 cup at a time, using just enough to make a medium, nonsticky dough. Rub the top of the dough with oil, cover and let it rise until doubled. Meanwhile make the filling.

Heat the oil in a saucepan and stir in the remaining ingredients. Stir to blend, and then remove from heat. When dough has doubled in bulk, punch it down and turn out onto a lightly floured bread board. Knead until it is elastic and no longer sticky. Roll it out to a 12- by 18-inch rectangle. Spread the filling over the rectangle of dough and then cut the dough into three 4-by 18-inch strips. Roll each of these strips into a long rope, pinching the ends closed and sealing all the edges. Place the strips on a buttered cookie sheet, seam sides down, and press the strips together at one end to form the top of the braid. Then carefully braid the 3 strips together, keeping the seams on the inside when possible. When finished with the braid, press the ends together and tuck them under just a little. Now cover with a cloth and let rise again until dough is light and has doubled in size. Bake in a preheated 350° F oven for 30 to 45 minutes, or until the loaf is golden brown and done. Brush with melted butter as soon as you take the loaf from the oven.

Makes 1 large loaf.

Zesty Sourdough Bread

This bread develops more zest than usual because the batter is allowed to stand so long. The extra sour taste is only for real sourdough buffs. Please read Success Tips before beginning.

1 cup sourdough starter	2 tablespoons sugar
1 cup lukewarm water	1 tablespoon salt
2 cups stirred and measured white flour	2 more cups stirred and measured white flour

In a large bowl combine the starter, water and 2 cups flour. Stir together until thoroughly mixed. Cover and let stand for 24 hours at least, up to 48 hours. At the end of that time, stir it down and add the remaining ingredients, using only enough of the flour to make a medium dough. Turn dough out onto a lightly floured board and knead it for 8 to 10 minutes, or until smooth and elastic. Shape into a round or long loaf and place on a buttered cookie sheet which has been sprinkled with corn meal. Cover and let rise until almost doubled, approximately 1 to 1-1/2 hours. Then bake in a preheated 400° F oven for 40 to 50 minutes, or until the top is browned and the bread tests done.

Jakes's Sourdough Bread

The best restaurant in Eastern Idaho serves a bread very similar to this. When I couldn't obtain the recipe, I set to work in my kitchen, and this bread is the result. It's a sturdy, delicious loaf that I usually make into rolls or small loaves. Please read Success Tips before beginning.

2 cups starter	2 cups stirred and measured whole wheat flour
2 cups lukewarm water	
1-1/2 cakes yeast	1 tablespoon salt
1/2 cup bulgur or cracked wheat soaked in 1/2 cup hot water	5 cups stirred and measured white or unbleached white flour
1/2 cup bran	

Combine starter, water and yeast. Stir together thoroughly and let proof for 8 minutes. Add the soaked bulgur, bran, whole wheat flour and salt. Beat until smooth. If desired, you can let this sponge proof for 30 minutes, or until light and bubbly. At the end of the proofing period, add the white flour, 1 cup at a time, until you have a medium-firm dough. Turn the dough out onto a lightly floured surface and knead until smooth and elastic.

When dough has been kneaded enough, turn it into a greased bowl and turn the dough so that it is greased all over. Cover and let rise until doubled in bulk, about 1-1/2 hours. Punch the dough down and shape it into 2 loaves to fit into 9-by 5-by 3-inch loaf pans, or into 3 or 4 dozen rolls, depending on size, or into 8 small loaves. Place in greased pans, cover and let rise until doubled in bulk. The time needed will depend on how the dough has been shaped. The large loaves will need at least an hour. The rolls and small loaves will be doubled in 30 to 45 minutes.

Bake in a preheated 375° F oven until browned and done. This will take an hour, or a little longer for the large loaves, while the rolls will be done in 25 to 30 minutes, and the small loaves in 30 to 40 minutes.

Sourdough Wheat Flakes Bread

This tasty bread came about when I had more starter than there was room for in the crock. So I began adding ingredients, and ended up with a very heavy, but very chewy and delicious bread. At first I just added wheat flakes to the sourdough along with some water and yeast and enough flour to make a medium dough. Then I started working with the recipe, and, while I wouldn't recommend it to anyone who likes the soft type of bread, it *is* good. *I very often omit the buttermilk salad dressing mix. However, it gives the bread a little more sour flavor which some people enjoy.* Please read Success Tips before beginning.

2 cups starter	1 package buttermilk salad
1-1/2 cups whole wheat flakes	dressing mix
2 cups lukewarm water	1 tablespoon salt
2 tablespoons sugar	3-1/2 cups stirred and measured
2 cakes yeast	white or unbleached
	white flour

Combine starter, wheat flakes, water and sugar and let stand for 15 minutes to soften the wheat flakes. Now stir in the yeast and let mixture set for 5 to 8 minutes to allow yeast to proof. Then stir in the salad dressing mix, salt, and the flour, adding the flour 1 cup at a time just until you have a medium dough. Turn the dough out onto a very lightly floured bread board and knead lightly. When dough has been kneaded, rub it all over with a little oil, place in a clean bowl, cover and let rise until doubled, approximately 2 hours.

When dough has doubled, punch it down and shape into 1 large loaf, or into 2 small loaves which fit into 8-inch bread pans. Cover pans and let dough rise again until doubled, and then bake in a preheated 350° F oven for 45 to 55 minutes, or until lightly browned and done.

Makes 1 or 2 loaves.

Joanne Booth's Sourdough Bread

Besides being city editor of the local newspaper, Joanne Booth is a good cook. Bread baking is one of her favorite hobbies, and this tasty bread is a result of her experiments in the kitchen. My family loved it. Please read Success Tips before beginning.

3/4 cup milk	1/2 cup wheat germ
1 cup hot water	3/4 cup any sourdough starter
1 large egg, beaten	3 tablespoons honey or brown
1 cake yeast	sugar
2 cups stirred and measured	1 tablespoon salt
white or unbleached	3 tablespoons vegetable oil
white flour	1 teaspoon baking soda
5 cups stirred and measured	sesame seeds
whole wheat flour	

Combine milk, water, and egg. Cool to 110° F. Add yeast and let proof 5 minutes. Stir in the white flour, 1-1/2 cups of the whole wheat flour, the wheat germ and the starter. Beat thoroughly, then cover and let rise until thick and spongy, about 1-1/2 to 2 hours.

At the end of that time, stir the sponge down and add the honey, salt, oil, and baking soda. Add remaining flour, 1 cup at a time, until it forms a firm dough. Turn dough out onto a floured surface and knead, adding just enough white or whole wheat flour so that the dough is not sticky.

Turn dough out into an oiled bowl and turn the dough so that the surface is covered with a thin film of oil. Cover and let rise until doubled in bulk, about 1-1/2 to 2 hours.

When dough has risen, punch it down and divide into 2 parts. Form each part into a loaf and place in well-greased 8-inch pans. Cover and let rise until nearly doubled, but not quite. Brush loaves with beaten egg white if desired, and sprinkle with sesame seeds. Bake in a 375° F oven about 35 to 40 minutes, or until loaves are well browned and test done. Turn out of pans and onto racks to cool. Makes 2 loaves.

Sourdough Cornbread

This makes a delicious cornbread to go with baked beans or a barbecue or some fried chicken. Occasionally I sprinkle some grated Cheddar or Jack cheese over the cornbread about 10 minutes before it is done.

4 slices thick bacon, diced and fried until crisp	1 cup corn meal
1/4 cup finely minced onions	2 tablespoons sugar
1 cup sourdough starter	1/4 cup stirred and measured white or unbleached white
1/2 cup buttermilk	flour
2 large eggs, beaten	1 teaspoon salt
1/4 cup bacon drippings or vegetable oil	2 teaspoons baking soda

Set aside the bacon and onions. Combine liquid ingredients and beat together. Stir together the dry ingredients. Add the liquid ingredients and stir together until thoroughly blended. Stir in the bacon and onions and pour mixture into a greased 7- by 11-inch baking pan. Bake in a 375° F oven for 30 to 40 minutes, or until bread is done.

Sourdough Cinnamon Rolls

Some people especially enjoy the tang of sourdough blended with some sweet ingredient. This is a good recipe, and the dough can be used as a basic sweet dough and thus varied as you wish. Please read Success Tips before beginning.

1-1/2 cups stirred and measured white flour	1/2 teaspoon baking soda
1/2 cup sugar	1 cup starter
1 teaspoon salt	1 large egg, beaten
1 teaspoon baking powder	1/2 cup melted butter or margarine

Combine dry ingredients in a mixing bowl and stir them together. Make a well in the center and pour the liquid ingredients into the well. Stir together until a thick dough is formed.

Turn this sticky dough out onto a lightly floured board and knead for 5 to 8 minutes, adding a little more flour if necessary to make a smooth, elastic dough. Then, without letting the dough rise, roll it out to a thickness of about 1/2 inch. Sprinkle with some cinnamon and brown sugar and dot with butter. Roll up and cut into 1/2-inch rolls. Place, cut side down, on a greased cookie sheet, cover and let rise for 1 hour, or until doubled. Bake in a preheated 350° F oven for 20 minutes or until browned and done. Make a glaze with powdered sugar and any desired liquid and brush on the hot rolls several times.

Honey-Orange Sourdough Rolls

I don't usually like sourdough sweet rolls or the cakes and doughnuts that are such a rage now. There seems to me to be a conflict between the zesty sourdough flavor and the sweet. However, these rolls are good. They're given an A rating by the friends and family I've made them for, and I even enjoy them myself. Please read Success Tips before beginning.

1 cake yeast
1/4 cup lukewarm water
1/2 cup milk
1/2 cup sourdough starter
1/2 teaspoon salt

1/4 cup melted butter or margarine
1/4 cup honey
3-1/4 cups white flour, stirred and measured

Orange-Nut Filling

1/2 cup butter or margarine
1/2 cup firmly packed brown sugar
1 tablespoon grated orange rind
1 teaspoon orange extract

1/4 cup honey
1/2 cup flour, stirred and measured
1/2 cup sliced almonds or other nuts

First make the dough. Soften the yeast in the water and then stir in the milk, starter, butter, honey, and salt. Gradually mix in enough of the flour (approximately 3 cups) to make a moderately soft, sticky dough. Rub the dough all over with oil and turn into a clean bowl.

Cover and let rise until doubled. While the dough is rising combine the ingredients for the filling and set aside.

When dough has doubled, punch it down and turn out onto a lightly floured bread board and knead until it is smooth and elastic, adding a little more flour if necessary to keep the dough from sticking.

Roll the dough out into a 12- by 15-inch rectangle. Spread the filling evenly over the dough. Starting with the long side, roll up in jelly roll fashion. Cut across the roll in about 1-inch thick slices and arrange, cut side up, in a well-greased 9- by 13- by 2-inch baking pan. Cover and let rise until almost but not quite doubled, about 45 minutes. Bake in a preheated 350° F oven for 35 minutes, or until browned on top. Transfer the hot rolls to a serving platter, scrape out any remaining syrup in the pan and pour it over the rolls. Serve warm. Makes 15 rolls.

English Sourdough Muffins

There must be twenty or more different recipes for English muffins. I've tried a number of them, but this one was the favorite with my test panel. Be sure to read Success Tips before beginning.

2 cakes yeast	4 teaspoons salt
2 cups lukewarm water	1 cup starter
1/2 cup skim milk crystals	6 cups stirred and measured
1/2 cup salad oil, melted	white or unbleached white
butter, or margarine	flour
1 tablespoon sugar	1/2 cup corn meal

Combine yeast, water and milk crystals. Set aside to proof for 5 to 8 minutes. Then stir in the salad oil, sugar, salt, starter and 2 cups of the flour. Stir together thoroughly and then add the remaining flour, 1 cup at a time, until you have a stiff dough. Turn this dough out onto a lightly floured board and knead until smooth and elastic, approximately 8 to 10 minutes. Rub the dough all over with oil, turn into a clean bowl, cover with a towel and let rise until doubled. When dough has doubled (about 1 hour depending on how warm the room is) punch it down, turn it back out onto the floured board and let the dough rest for 10 minutes. Then roll out to a thickness of 1/2 inch and cut into 3-inch rounds. Place the muffins on a greased baking sheet which has been sprinkled with corn meal, sprinkle the top with more cornmeal, cover the sheet of muffins and let rise until puffy and light, about 15 to 20 minutes.

Now preheat a griddle or electric frying pan to 375° F, carefully lift (using a spatula) the patties onto the ungreased griddle and bake for 10 to 12 minutes, or until golden brown and done, turning once so that each side is baked and browned. Cool on a rack. Split and serve.

Note. These freeze very well. Simply split them first, package and freeze. They can be reheated in the toaster.

Delicious Sourdough Biscuits

There are probably a hundred versions of sourdough biscuits, each of them differing only slightly from the rest. I gave a recipe in *A World of Breads* that I thought was the best. Now, however, we prefer this one. Please read Success Tips before beginning.

1 cake yeast	1-1/2 teaspoons salt
1/3 cup sugar	5 cups stirred and measured
2 cups lukewarm water	flour
1 cup basic starter	

Place yeast in a mixing bowl. Add sugar and water and stir to dissolve the yeast. Let the yeast proof for 5 to 8 minutes. Then add the starter, salt and flour. Stir to mix thoroughly. Cover the bowl with plastic wrap and let it rise until doubled.

When the dough has doubled in volume, turn it out onto a lightly floured bread board and roll or pat it to a square or rectangle that is 3/4 inch thick. Cut into biscuits. Place on a buttered baking pan, brush tops with salad oil, cover the pan and let the biscuits rise again until almost, but not quite, doubled. Bake in a preheated 425° F oven for 15 to 20 minutes, or until golden brown and done. Brush tops with a little butter or margarine and serve hot.

Sourdough Whole Wheat Biscuits

If you like you can make these with all white flour, but the whole wheat flour adds more flavor. Be sure to read Success Tips before beginning.

1 cup stirred and measured whole wheat flour	2 teaspoons baking powder
1 cup stirred and measured white flour	1/2 teaspoon salt
	1/2 cup butter or margarine
	2 cups sourdough starter

Measure dry ingredients into a mixing bowl and stir together. Cut the butter in until it is in lumps the size of small peas. Then stir in the starter.

Turn dough onto a very lightly floured board and knead very, very lightly, just enough so that the ingredients hold together. This is always the secret of tender biscuits. If the dough is too sticky you may need to use a little more flour. Roll dough out to a thickness of 1/2 inch and cut with a biscuit cutter. Place on a buttered cookie sheet and let rise, covered, for 30 minutes.

Bake in a preheated 425° F oven for 20 to 25 minutes, or until biscuits are lightly browned and done.

Dunham's Pancakes

Chuck and Mary Dunham begin all of their varied sourdough recipes with this basic pancake batter. To the leftover batter they add an assortment of flours and/or other ingredients to make an array of sourdough breads, all of which are taste treats. The Dunhams are very casual about exact amounts. They recommend that people experiment until they find their own favorite way of making pancakes and other sourdough products. What they offer in this and other recipes of theirs throughout this chapter is a suggestion, a way of using sourdough that has certainly proven both effective and delicious. They never use any yeast in their sourdough recipes, claiming that if the starter is good and active, extra yeast is unnecessary. These pancakes are so light and fluffy that they almost float, and the waffles are so crisp that you think they might shatter. Please read Success Tips before beginning.

2-1/2 cups stirred and measured white flour	1/4 cup reconstituted dry milk or scalded and cooled fresh milk
2 cups lukewarm water	
1 cup starter	1/2 teaspoon baking soda
2 large eggs	1/2 teaspoon salt
2 tablespoons salad oil, melted butter, or margarine	1 tablespoon sugar

Begin the evening before by making a sponge with the flour, water and starter. Stir all together, cover the bowl and let the batter work overnight. It should have, for best flavor, at least 8 and preferably 12 hours.

In the morning remove 1 cup of the starter and reserve for the next batch. To the remaining sponge add the eggs, salad oil, and milk. Beat well until all ingredients are blended and the mixture is uniform. If the sponge should happen to be a little too stiff, add a little milk or water to thin to the proper consistency. If it is too fluid add a little more flour.

Combine the baking soda, salt, and sugar in a small cup and sprinkle over the top of the batter. Fold it in carefully but thoroughly. The batter will expand and nearly double in size. Bake the pancakes on a preheated greased griddle, allowing a little extra time as sourdough pancakes don't bake as quickly as regular pancakes. Serve topped with crushed fresh fruit or any other desired topping.

SOURDOUGH WAFFLES. To make crisp, thin waffles add an extra 2 tablespoons salad oil or melted shortening and 1/2 cup milk. For extra lightness, separate the eggs, stir the yolks into the batter with the milk, beat the whites until stiff, and then fold them into the batter with the baking soda mixture.

Note. Any remaining pancake or waffle batter may be stored in the refrigerator and used later as is. However, the Dunhams consider the leftover batter as a "planned over," for this is where their creativity comes in.

SOURDOUGH ROLLS. Take any amount of leftover batter, and to it add enough white flour to make a soft dough. Turn out onto a lightly floured board and knead in enough more flour to make a barely medium dough. It should not be sticky, however. Shape the dough into rolls, greasing your hands so that the dough doesn't stick. Place on a greased pan and let rise until doubled in bulk. Bake in a preheated 400° F oven for 15 to 20 minutes, or until golden brown and done.

BREAD. Make as above only shape in one or more loaves and place in greased bread pan. Let rise until not quite doubled in bulk. Bake in a preheated 375° F oven for 45 minutes, or until loaves test done.

EASY POTATO BREAD. Mary adds a tablespoon or more of potato flakes or granules to the "planned over" batter. Stir it in and let set for a few minutes. Then add white flour as above to make into either rolls or bread. Let rise and bake as above.

RYE BREAD. This is excellent. Similar to the common bread that is baked in European countries, it is dark, heavy, and full of rich flavor. Take leftover batter and stir in rye flour until you can no longer stir. Let the dough rest for a few minutes, and then if it is sticky, add a little white flour until dough is no longer sticky when you slap it with your hand. Shape into long, thin loaves, or into buns. Let it rise until it "seems to stop," according to Mary, and then proceed as in the above recipes.

SOURDOUGH BREAD STICKS. Add white flour to the leftover batter to form a stiff dough. Let the dough relax for about 10 minutes and then divide the dough into small balls. Roll these balls out on a very lightly floured board to form long, thin sticks, keeping in mind the fact that the finished product will be about 3 times thicker after it has risen and been baked. Place these sticks on a lightly greased cookie sheet, cover and let rise until doubled in bulk. Brush with slightly beaten egg white and sprinkle with coarse salt or with poppy or sesame seeds. Bake in a preheated 400° F oven for 15 minutes, or until golden brown and done. Cool on a rack. Store in a dry spot, and reheat slightly before serving.

SOURDOUGH OATMEAL BREAD. This has an excellent nutty flavor and makes delicious toast. Add approximately 1/4 cup regular or instant oats to 2 cups of leftover pancake batter. Let set for an hour, and then stir in just enough stirred and measured white flour, 1 cup at a time, until you have a medium, non-sticky dough. Turn the dough out onto a lightly floured board and knead lightly. Turn into a greased bread pan, cover and let rise until it is almost doubled. Bake in a preheated 375° F oven until browned and done, approximately 35 to 45 minutes.

PULL-APARTS. Use any of the bread variations and form the dough into thin patties with a light greasing on all sides. Place these patties on edge in a greased bread pan. Let rise and bake according to variation instructions. When baked it will look like a regular loaf, but will pull apart easily.

Chuck Dunham's Caraway Rye Bread

I've mentioned Chuck and Mary Dunham before in this chapter. This is another of their excellent breads. Please read Success Tips before beginning.

1 quart leftover batter from	2 tablespoons cocoa
Dunham's Pancakes	1/4 teaspoon salt
1 tablespoon dark corn syrup	1 tablespoon caraway seed
1-1/2 to 2 cups rye flour	

Combine all ingredients with the exception of the flour. Mix just enough for uniform distribution of ingredients. Add just enough of the flour to make a dough that can be shaped. Knead lightly. Form into long, narrow loaves and place on a buttered and corn-mealed cookie sheet, or in baguette pans that have been buttered and corn mealed.

Cover the loaves and allow to rise until not quite doubled. Bake for 50 minutes in a preheated 375° F oven, or until browned and done. Brush the loaves with butter after removing from the oven. Makes 2 small loaves.

Note. The Dunhams occasionally add 1/4 cup of instant potato flakes to the leftover pancake batter before adding the remaining ingredients.

Dunham's Norwegian Christmas Sourdough Bread

Before beginning, please read Success Tips at the start of this chapter.

1 quart leftover batter from	1/2 teaspoon vanilla extract
Dunham's Pancakes	3/4 cup glacé fruit
grated rind and juice of 1 orange	1/4 cup raisins or currants
seeds from 3 whole cardamom,	stirred and measured white or
pounded into 1 teaspoon	unbleached white flour to
sugar	make a soft, moist dough

Combine all ingredients except for the flour. Add the flour, 1 cup at a time, using just enough to make a soft, moist dough. Shape the dough into flattened balls and place in a greased, round layer cake pan. Cover and let rise until nearly doubled in bulk. Bake in a preheated 375° F oven for 45 minutes, or until golden brown and done. Cool on a rack and when cooled, glaze with mixture of sifted powdered sugar and orange juice. Decorate, if desired, with slivered, blanched almonds or more glacé fruit.

Sourdough Pancakes

These are absolutely fantastic, and very simple. Please read Success Tips before beginning.

2 cups any sourdough starter	2 eggs
1 tablespoon sugar	2 tablespoons salad oil, melted
1 teaspoon salt	butter, or margarine

1 teaspoon baking soda

Mix all ingredients together and bake pancakes on a greased hot griddle until done, turning once. Serve with real maple syrup, if possible. Serves four.

Sourdough Blueberry Pancakes

Although I don't very often allow myself the privilege of eating pancakes, when I do indulge I want them perfect. And this means beginning with a good recipe, cooking them properly and then serving them with warm melted butter, and *hot* syrup. Cold syrup on hot pancakes is appalling! With these very good pancakes I serve either a hot maple syrup or blueberry syrup. Please read Success Tips before beginning.

1 cup starter	2 tablespoons salad oil, melted
2 cups lukewarm water	butter, or margarine
2-1/2 cups stirred and	1/2 cup milk
measured flour	1 teaspoon baking soda
2 large eggs, beaten	1 cup fresh or frozen
2 tablespoons sugar	blueberries or
	huckleberries

The evening before, mix the starter with the lukewarm water and flour. Cover and let stand overnight. Do not refrigerate. In the morning stir the sponge down and add the remaining ingredients. Let the batter stand for 10 to 15 minutes, then bake pancakes on a hot, greased griddle.

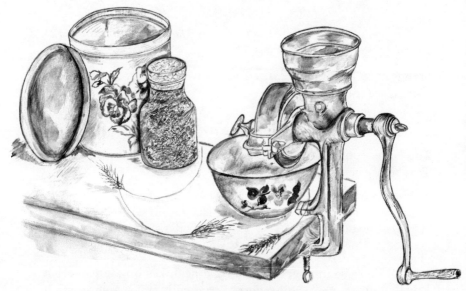

Whole Wheat
Breads

BREAD has been considered "the staff of life" for thousands of years. However, for a time our society's penchant for soft, cottony white breads certainly suggested that the staff was, if not broken, at least badly bent. But within the past decade there has been an increasing interest in making breads "from scratch" and coming up with a final product that not only looks good and is full of flavor, but is also *good for you.*

I see this new attitude every time I give a demonstration to a group of bakers. No longer do they raise their eyebrows or express polite disinterest when I suggest using soy flour, skim milk powder, wheat germ and other enriching products. And no longer do people want a "whole wheat" bread that is mainly white flour, simply colored with a little whole wheat flour. I know many people who won't buy white flour, but use whole wheat or some other whole grain flour for virtually everything.

Theoretically you can take any bread recipe and convert it to a whole wheat or whole grain recipe simply by using brown sugar or molasses for the sweetening, and substituting whole wheat or graham flour for part or all of the white flour. It doesn't, however, always work out as well that way. White flour gives a lighter, fluffier, finer textured bread, and some recipes require white flour for that reason. Some of the more delicate, beautiful, and airy breads and rolls, like *Brioche* or *Croissants*, are simply not the same when made with a whole grain flour. For this reason it is best to use recipes that are formulated for whole wheat or graham flour, or a white flour recipe that states specifically that you can make certain whole grain substitutions.

Success Tips for Whole Wheat Breads

Flour. Remember that whole wheat flour and graham flour are always interchangeable. Neither the whole wheat nor the graham flour should be sifted. Stir the flour and then spoon it lightly into a cup. Level the top by running a knife edge across it. Do not shake the cup or pack the flour.

To Eliminate the First Rising and Some Kneading. You can eliminate the first rising and cut the kneading time in any whole wheat bread by combining 1 cup of the flour with 1-1/2 cups of the liquid and cooking and stirring it together until thick and smooth. At first the mixture will be lumpy, but it will smooth out in the cooking. When cooked, turn the mixture out into the mixing bowl, cool just a bit and then add the remaining ingredients. Continue as directed in the recipe. This method is quite effective.

Sweetening. You can use brown sugar, honey or molasses in any whole grain recipe. They are all interchangeable. Molasses, especially the blackstrap, has the strongest flavor — a point to keep in mind if you are using 1/2 cup or so. We prefer honey. With the molasses or honey you might need a little more flour. Always use just enough flour to make a medium soft, or stiff, dough.

Milk. In any breads which call for milk, I find it much easier to use skim milk powder, and stir it in with the flour. You can increase the nutritional value immensely by this method. For example, if a recipe calls for 2 cups of milk, I use 2 cups of water and enough milk *powder* to make 1 quart of milk. This process increases the protein and calcium substantially, and the milk tastes rich but has no more calories than 2 cups of whole milk. It doesn't affect the other ingredients in any way. And there is no fat.

Other Liquid Ingredients. If a recipe calls for plain water, you can use potato water if desired. I sometimes use a mild broth, such as chicken, when making dinner breads or rolls. This is especially good when combined with 1/2 teaspoon of a favorite herb.

Kneading. To knead properly, you simply press down and away from you, then fold the dough in half, give it a quarter turn and press down again. Continue pressing, folding and turning, until the dough is smooth and elastic.

Rising. Whole wheat breads take longer to rise than do white breads, sometimes as much as twice as long. The rising time always depends on how much yeast is used, how light or heavy the dough is, and how warm your kitchen is. If the weather is quite cold you can set the bowl of dough over a pan of hot water to rise.

Shaping the Loaves. Whole wheat bread is better when baked in small loaves rather than large ones. And the texture is improved by twisting the dough. For this reason I braid most whole wheat breads, even when I bake them in pans. If you don't want to braid the loaves, just cut each loaf into 2 pieces and twist these together. The loaves look nice when baked, and the texture is still improved. If you wish to braid the loaves to bake on a cookie sheet, then you need to add just a little more flour to make a slightly firmer dough. This helps to maintain the shape while baking.

Pans. Whatever kind of pans you use, brush them with melted margarine or lard rather than with oil. The oil is absorbed into the dough and does not do a good job of providing a non-stick surface.

Freezing. All breads freeze very well as long as they are properly wrapped. After baking, let the loaves cool completely. Place in freezer bags and seal. Freeze for up to 3 months. Thaw at room temperature, or remove from bag, wrap in foil and thaw in a 325° F oven for 20 to 30 minutes. I do not recommend thawing in a microwave oven as it sometimes toughens the bread. For small families, I strongly recommend slicing the bread first and freezing in each package only as many slices as you would use in a day or two. In this way you can enjoy homemade bread without worrying about wasting any.

Nutritional Note. You can pack some nutritional dynamite in every loaf of bread you bake with the simple addition of soy flour, wheat germ, and the skim milk powder already discussed. In any average recipe using 6 to 8 cups of flour, substitute 1/4 cup *each* of soy flour and wheat germ for 1/2 cup of the flour used in the recipe. Soy flour lacks the gluten needed to develop yeast doughs, so it cannot be used alone. However, it contains 15 times as much calcium and 10 times as much iron as regular flour, as well as being a highly concentrated protein food. I highly recommend its regular use.

To Use the Microwave Oven. Whole grain breads are perfect for the microwave oven because they don't need to brown. If you want you can let the bread dough rise in the oven, allowing 15 to 20 minutes on the #2 setting for both variable or solid state ovens. To bake, use the #5 setting, and bake for 6 to 8 minutes.

Whole Wheat Bread

Like most breads, this can be varied extensively. I sometimes use graham flour instead of whole wheat flour. Occasionally I brush the entire loaf with beaten egg white and roll it in sesame seeds before placing in a greased bread pan. When I want the bread to be crunchy I knead in 1/2 to 3/4 cup softened cracked wheat, or soy grits; and sometimes I knead in 1/2 to 1 cup of leftover mashed potatoes or any leftover cooked cereal, adding a bit more flour if necessary. And I occasionally substitute for a cup of the flour one of the following: a cup of soy or rye flour; bran flakes; rice polish or corn meal. Use 1/2 cup gluten flour to keep the dough light. Please read Success Tips before beginning.

1/2 cup lukewarm water	1/4 cup melted butter or
1/4 to 1/2 cup brown sugar,	margarine, or vegetable
molasses, or honey	oil
2 cakes yeast	2 teaspoons salt
2-1/2 cups lukewarm water	7 to 8 cups stirred and measured
	whole wheat flour

Combine 1/2 cup water, brown sugar and yeast. Proof for 5 minutes. Then add remaining water, butter, salt and 3 cups of the flour. Beat with a wooden spoon until mixture forms a smooth batter.

Add remaining flour, 1 cup at a time, using just enough to make a medium firm dough. Turn dough out onto a lightly floured bread board and knead until it is smooth and elastic. Add more flour as needed to prevent sticking.

Turn dough into a greased bowl, turning the dough so that it is greased all over. Cover and let rise until doubled in bulk, approximately 1 hour.

When dough has doubled, punch it down, cover and let rise again. After the second rising, punch dough down and shape into 2 loaves. Place in greased bread pans, cover and let rise until not quite doubled in bulk.

Bake in a preheated 350° F oven for 50 to 60 minutes, or until loaves test done. Cool on racks. Makes 2 loaves.

100% Whole Wheat Bread

This bread will take longer to rise than a white bread. But it is tasty and filling, worth waiting for. If you use the larger amount of yeast it will rise a bit faster.

1 or 2 cakes yeast	1/4 cup brown sugar or honey
1-1/2 cups lukewarm water	1/4 cup margarine, lard, or oil
1-1/2 cups milk	6 to 7 cups unsifted whole
1 tablespoon salt	wheat or graham flour

Dissolve the yeast in the lukewarm water. Scald the milk and pour over the salt, sugar and margarine. Stir until sugar is dissolved and margarine melted. Cool to lukewarm. This should take just a few minutes. When it is cooled to lukewarm, add the yeast mixture. Now stir in half of the flour and beat with a spoon until the batter is smooth. Then begin adding the remaining flour slowly, until you have a medium stiff dough. When the dough is stiff enough to handle, turn it out onto a lightly floured bread board. Knead thoroughly, adding just enough flour so that the dough is not sticky.

When the dough has been kneaded enough so that it is elastic, spread it with oil or melted margarine and turn into a clean bowl. Cover and let rise until doubled. This will take from 1 to 3 hours, depending on the amount of yeast used, and on the warmth of your kitchen. When the dough has doubled, punch it down and turn it out onto a *very* lightly floured or oiled bread board. Cut into 2 pieces and mold each piece into a loaf shape. Turn into oiled or buttered 9-inch loaf pans, cover and let rise again until double. This will take from 45 minutes to 1-1/2 hours. Bake in a preheated 325° F oven for 1 to 1-1/2 hours, or until loaves test done. Makes 2 loaves.

Note. If you want, you may use all water — 3 cups in all — instead of half water and half milk. This gives more of the flavor of the wheat. Or you can use all water and stir 1/2 to 3/4 cup skim milk *powder* in with the flour. This adds much greater nutrition. For a still greater nutritional wallop, you can replace 2 cups of the flour with 1 cup each of soy flour and wheat germ.

WHOLE WHEAT RAISIN BREAD. To make a not too sweet but delicious raisin bread, especially good toasted, simply stir in 1 tablespoon cinnamon and 1 cup raisins.

TO FREEZE. See page 126.

Basic Whole Grain Bread

This is a basic and delicious bread. It is my favorite of the many whole wheat breads. We especially enjoy the many variations, our particular favorites being the Sesame Seed Bread and the Cheese Bread. Flavor and density will depend on the flour or meal used, but kneading is a very important factor in whole grain breads. So be sure to knead for at least 8 to 10 minutes.

2 cakes yeast

1/3 cup brown sugar, honey, or molasses

3 cups lukewarm water

8 to 9 cups whole wheat or graham flour, with some extra for kneading

1 cup skim milk *powder*

1 tablespoon salt

1/3 cup melted margarine or lard, or salad oil

Dissolve the yeast and sugar in 1 cup of the lukewarm water. Set aside for 5 minutes, or until it bubbles and begins to foam. Then stir into the remaining 2 cups of water in a large bowl. Now beat in 4 cups of the flour and the skim milk powder. Beat with a wooden spoon until smooth. This is your sponge. Cover it with a clean towel and set aside until it doubles approximately 30 to 45 minutes.

When the sponge has risen, stir it down and beat in the salt, oil, and enough of the remaining flour to make a dough that leaves the sides of the bowl. Turn out onto a *very* lightly floured bread board and knead thoroughly, adding more flour if needed, but just enough to keep the dough from sticking. You should knead the dough for at least 8 to 10 minutes. Then oil the dough all over and turn into a bowl. Cover and let rise until doubled. This will take about 45 minutes. At the end of that time, punch the dough down and let it rise for another 30 minutes. At the end of that time, punch the dough down again and turn out onto a *very* lightly floured, or oiled, board and cut into 2 pieces. Shape each piece into a loaf and place in oiled or buttered standard 9-inch loaf pans. Cover and let rise 30 minutes, or until barely doubled. Bake in a preheated 350° F oven for 45 minutes to an hour, or until bread tests done. Remove from pans and cool on rack.

Note. For a lighter loaf you can replace half of the flour with unbleached white flour, or with all-purpose flour.

RYE-OAT BREAD. For a darker bread use molasses instead of honey or sugar. Replace the whole wheat flour with the following: 2 cups white flour, 4 cups rye flour, 2 cups old fashioned rolled oats.

LIGHT RYE BREAD. Replace 1 cup of the water with 1/2 cup buttermilk or sour milk and 3 large eggs. Use a total of 3 cups white flour and 5 to 6 cups rye flour. Add 3 to 4 tablespoons of caraway seeds.

DARK RYE BREAD. Use molasses instead of honey or sugar. Substitute 1 cup of sour cream or yogurt for 1 cup of the water. Use 5 or 6 cups of rye flour and the rest whole wheat. Add 2 or 3 tablespoons caraway seeds.

CHEESE BREAD. To the basic dough add 2 cups grated Cheddar cheese, preferably a sharp Cheddar. Add 3 large eggs to the sponge, beating them in. Add the cheese with the final addition of flour before kneading.

OATMEAL BREAD. Use either brown sugar or honey. Use a total of the following: 2 cups white flour, 3 cups old fashioned rolled oats, 4 to 4-1/2 cups whole wheat or graham flour.

SESAME SEED BREAD. Use brown sugar or honey. Use a total of the following: 3 cups white flour, 4 cups whole wheat or graham flour, 3 cups sesame seed meal, 1 cup cracked millet. If you don't live near a health food store, you can make sesame seed meal from whole sesame seeds, and cracked millet from whole millet, in your blender.

Note. 1 or 1-1/2 cups of raisins or chopped nuts, or a combination of the two, can be added to the dough. Or you can use some chopped dried apricots, peaches or apples which have been soaked until they are softened.

Two-Hour Whole Wheat Bread

Actually this 100% whole wheat bread can be made in less than 2 hours, from start to finish. However, you do need some kind of a bread mixer to develop the gluten in a short period of time. It's a good, heavy bread, especially good with home ground whole wheat flour. Be sure to read Success Tips before beginning.

2 cakes yeast	7 cups stirred and measured
1/4 cup honey	whole wheat flour
4 cups lukewarm water	1 tablespoon salt

Dissolve the yeast and the honey in the warm water. Add the flour and salt and beat in a heavy-duty mixer for 5 to 10 minutes.

Turn the dough, which will be more of a heavy batter than a dough, into 2 greased standard loaf pans. Smooth the tops with wet hands. Cut a slit down the middle of each loaf with a sharp knife. Set in a warm place and cover. Let rise until light, but not doubled, approximately 20 minutes. Bake in a preheated 350° F oven for 50 to 60 minutes, or until the loaves are done. This is best eaten while still warm.

   Makes 2 loaves.

Uncle Reed's Famous Blue Ribbon Whole Wheat Bread

This excellent recipe is from Idaho Falls farmer Reed Hansen, who says that he actually won the blue ribbon for his sourdough bread. However, this recipe is worthy of a blue ribbon in any state fair. Please read Success Tips before beginning.

1/2 cup lukewarm water	10 or 12 potatoes, cooked and
2 teaspoons sugar	mashed, peel and all
2 cakes yeast	3-1/2 cups of the potato
1 tablespoon salt	water, cooled to
1 tablespoon sugar	lukewarm
2 tablespoons molasses, brown	2 cups rye flour, stirred and
sugar, or honey	measured
2 tablespoons salad oil or	2 cups whole wheat flour,
melted butter or	stirred and measured
margarine	2 cups bran buds
3/4 cup undiluted evaporated	5 or 6 cups white flour, stirred
milk	and measured

Combine the first 3 ingredients and set aside to proof for 5 to 8 minutes. Then stir in the remaining ingredients up to and including the potato water. Stir all together. Then add the rye flour, whole wheat flour and bran buds. Stir all together.

   When the mixture is thoroughly blended, begin adding the white flour 1 cup at a time, using only enough to make a medium dough. Turn the dough out onto a lightly floured bread board and knead for 8 to 10 minutes. Hansen says, "I beat the dickens out of the dough, unleashing all of my frustrations. When I'm tired of beating the stuff, I cut it into 4 parts, shape it into loaves and place in greased 9-inch bread pans."

   Cover the loaves and let them rise again. Bake in a preheated 400° F oven for 10 minutes, and then at 350° F for 30 minutes, "give or take 5 or 10 minutes." Hansen finished this recipe with the comment that "If you have generally followed directions, you will have some of the finest bread in the west. Now sit down, take a break, and enjoy it."

Whole Wheat French Bread

This is a good "French type" bread. The gluten flour helps give the texture that we most admire in this type of bread. Baked in baquette pans, these make marvelous Hero or Poor Boy sandwiches. Please read Success Tips before starting.

1 or 2 cakes yeast	1 tablespoon salt
2 cups lukewarm water	1 cup unsifted gluten flour
1/2 teaspoon honey or brown sugar	2 cups whole wheat or graham flour
2 or 3 tablespoons olive or salad oil	1-1/2 to 2-1/2 cups white or unbleached white flour

Combine yeast, water, and honey or sugar in a large mixing bowl. Set aside until it bubbles. Then stir in the oil, salt, and gluten flour. Add the whole wheat flour and beat with a wooden spoon. Now, begin adding the white flour gradually, using just enough to make a medium stiff dough. Turn out on a very lightly floured bread board, and knead until smooth and elastic, using just enough flour so that the dough is not sticky. Remember that if you think you have used *too much* flour, spread the board with a little oil instead of flour.

When the dough has been kneaded enough, spread it with oil all over and place in a clean bowl. Cover with a towel and let rise until doubled. The time will depend on how warm the kitchen is and on how much yeast you have used. Allow for 1-1/2 to 2 hours. When the dough has doubled punch it down and turn out onto a very lightly *oiled* board. Cut into 2 pieces, cover the pieces and let rest for 10 to 15 minutes. Then shape each piece into a long loaf. Place on a cookie sheet that has been oiled and sprinkled with corn meal, or in oiled baquette pans that have been sprinkled with corn meal. Cover and let rise until doubled. Sometime during the rising, or at the end of the rising time, slash the tops with a razor blade or a *very* sharp knife. When doubled in bulk brush the loaves with cold water and sprinkle with coarse salt if desired. Place in a preheated 400° F oven. A pan of boiling water on the bottom of the oven will aid in achieving a crunchy crust. Bake until done, brushing several times with cold water. The loaves will take 40 to 50 minutes baking time. Cool on a rack.

Note. You might line the oven rack with tiles and slide the loaves onto the hot tiles to bake.

MIXED GRAIN FRENCH BREAD. For a deliciously crunchy loaf, use 1 cup each of whole wheat and graham flour, 1 cup softened cracked wheat and 1 cup white flour. If more flour is needed, use white flour.

Whole Wheat Sesame Seed Bread

This crunchy, hearty loaf is one of the best "health breads," if breads that are good for you *must* be labeled as such. The original recipe called for 45 minutes of kneading and a cup of sweetening, neither of which is necessary. *However, if you do not have a heavy duty mixer with a dough hook in which to mix the dough, I would recommend at least 15 minutes of hand kneading.* If you want, you might replace some of the whole wheat flour with bran flakes, or with some other whole grain flour. Please read Success Tips before starting.

1 12-1/2 ounce can goat's milk or plain evaporated milk	1 cup stirred and measured white or unbleached white flour
11-1/2 ounces water (to make 3 cups of liquid)	1 tablespoon salt
1/3 cup vegetable oil	1/2 to 3/4 cup cracked wheat
1/2 cup brown sugar, honey, or molasses	1/2 cup wheat germ
3 cakes yeast	1 to 2 cups additional white or unbleached white flour, stirred and measured
4 cups stirred and measured whole wheat flour	3/4 cup sesame seeds
	1 large egg, beaten

Combine liquids, vegetable oil and sweetening. Heat until barely lukewarm. Turn into a large bowl and add the yeast. Let sit for 5 minutes. Then stir in the whole wheat flour, the 1 cup of white flour, and the salt and mix with a heavy duty mixer for 5 minutes.

Add the cracked wheat and wheat germ and beat for 5 more minutes. Then add enough of the additional flour to make a medium firm dough and beat for 5 more minutes. Turn out onto a very lightly floured bread board and knead lightly for just a few minutes. Cover the dough with a clean towel and let it rest for 15 minutes.

When dough has rested for 15 minutes, punch it down and divide into 2 parts. Roll each part into a rectangle, sprinkle with 1/3 cup of sesame seeds and roll up tightly, pushing the edges together to form a compact loaf. Place in greased standard 9-inch bread pans, cover and let rise until almost, but not quite doubled, approximately 20 minutes.

Brush loaves with the beaten egg, sprinkle with the remaining sesame seeds and bake in a preheated 350° F oven until browned and done, approximately 45 minutes. Makes 2 loaves.

Whole Wheat Potato Bread

Wrapped and stored in your refrigerator, this bread will keep nicely for up to a week. And, like all breads, it freezes well. The variations are excellent.

1 medium potato, peeled and cut into cubes	1/2 cup skim milk *powder*
	1/4 cup brown sugar or honey
2 cups water	1 tablespoon salt
1 tablespoon brown sugar or honey	1/3 cup melted margarine or lard, or salad oil
2 cakes yeast	1 large egg
4-1/2 to 5-1/2 cups whole wheat or graham flour	

Combine water and potato in a small saucepan and cook until potato is tender. Drain, reserving the liquid, and mash the potato. Combine and add water as necessary to make 3 cups combined potato and liquid. Pour this into a large mixing bowl and cool, if necessary, to lukewarm. Then stir in the 1 tablespoon sugar or honey, and the yeast. Let stand a few minutes, then stir in half of the flour with the skim milk powder. Beat together until smooth and then beat in the 1/4 cup sugar or honey, salt, melted margarine or oil and the egg. Beat a little more, and then begin adding the remaining flour, stirring it in first with a spoon and then with your hands, until the mixture will take no more flour and is a medium dough. Spread a little more flour on a bread board and turn the dough out onto it. Knead gently, kneading in just enough flour to keep the dough from sticking. Now rub the dough all over with melted margarine or oil, and place in a bowl. Cover and let rise until doubled, approximately 1 to 1-1/2 hours.

When dough has doubled, punch it down and turn out onto a *very* lightly floured, or oiled, board and knead again for 2 or 3 minutes. Then, leaving the dough on the board, cover with a towel again, and let sit for 15 minutes. Knead again for another minute or two. The dough is now ready to be shaped. It can be braided into a lovely loaf (see instructions on page 126). Or it can be cut into 2 pieces, and each molded into a long or a round loaf shape on a buttered cookie sheet. Whichever way you do it, after the dough has been shaped and placed on the cookie sheet, cover it with a towel and let rise until doubled. Slash the top lightly with a razor blade, or a very sharp knife. Bake in a preheated 375° F oven for 30 to 35 minutes, or until loaves test done.

CHEESE BREAD. This variation is especially good when used with the Rye Bread variation. When dough is ready for shaping, divide it into 2 parts. Flatten each part and cover the dough with small cubes of Cheddar cheese. Now fold the dough over on itself several times, tightly, tuck the edges under and press together, forming into a loaf shape with your hands. Place on buttered cookie sheet, cover and let rise. Slash tops of loaves lightly and bake as directed. This makes delicious sandwiches.

RYE BREAD. Substitute 1-1/2 to 2 cups rye flour for the same amount of whole wheat, adding the rye flour towards the end. If you like caraway seeds, add 2 tablespoons to the dough. Shape the dough into long loaves and place on a buttered cookie sheet that has been sprinkled with corn meal. Just before the loaves go into the oven, slash the tops very lightly with a razor blade, or a very sharp knife.

ONION BREAD. This variation is very good combined with either the Rye, or the Cheese variation. Simply add a package of onion soup mix to the dough, dissolving it first in a tiny bit of hot water. Bake as directed above.

Whole Wheat Cuban Bread

This is crusty, delicious water bread, an excellent bread for beginners because it is so easy to make and the results are so satisfying. As it contains no shortening, this bread is best eaten the day it is made. It won't keep for more than a day or two. Like all breads, however, it freezes very well.

1 cake yeast	2 tablespoons salt
2 cups lukewarm water or potato water	4 cups whole wheat or graham flour
1 or 2 tablespoons brown sugar or honey	3 to 3-1/2 cups white flour

Dissolve the yeast and sugar in the lukewarm water. When dissolved, stir in the salt and the whole wheat flour. Beat until thoroughly blended together. Now begin adding the white flour, using just enough to make a medium dough. Turn out onto a *very* lightly floured bread board and knead, kneading in just enough flour to make a non-sticky dough. Spread the dough with oil and turn into a bowl to rise, covered, until doubled. This will take 1-1/2 to 2 hours. When the dough has doubled, punch it down and turn out onto a lightly *oiled* bread board. Cut into 2 parts and shape each into a loaf, either long or round. Place on an oiled cookie sheet that has been sprinkled with a little corn meal.

Cover the loaves and let rise again until almost, but not quite, doubled. Slash the tops with a razor blade, or a very sharp knife and pop into a *cold* oven. This is important. Set the oven at 400° and bake until bread is nicely browned and done, about 45 minutes. Brush the tops with cold water several times while baking.

CUBAN CRACKLING BREAD. After the dough has risen once, knead in 1 cup of crisp pork cracklings and 1 tablespoon *cracked* black pepper. Continue as directed above, only brush the dough with lard or bacon fat during baking.

Pita Bread

When I wrote my first book, *A World of Breads*, only those of Middle Eastern descent were familiar with Pita Bread. Since then this versatile and delicious bread has become so popular that it is sold in markets in virtually every large city in the nation. The top of this flat, round bread puffs up during the baking forming a natural pocket. The bread is marvelous simply buttered and eaten fresh and hot from the oven. But that natural pocket makes it extremely versatile. It's a natural for sandwiches. Sometimes I fill the pocket with cheese, tomato slices and thin slices of ham, sprinkle with a bit of oregano and pop into the oven until the cheese melts. It also is great for hamburgers, shish kebab and almost any good sandwich filling. In an Armenian restaurant we had Pita filled with chopped lettuce and *falafel* (a Middle Eastern *garbanzo* mixture), and another time with an Armenian hamburger (a delicious mixture of ground lamb, ground beef, minced onion, parsley, and seasoned salt).

Please read Success Tips before starting.

2 cakes yeast	1 to 1-1/2 tablespoons salt
1/2 teaspoon honey	3 cups white flour
2 cups lukewarm water	1-1/2 to 2 cups whole wheat or
1/4 cup olive or salad oil	graham flour

Dissolve the yeast and honey in the lukewarm water. Then add the oil, salt, and the 3 cups of white flour. Work these ingredients together with a wooden spoon. Now begin adding the whole wheat flour using just enough to make a medium, slightly sticky dough. If there is any flour left, spread this on the bread board. Turn the dough out onto the floured board and knead in just enough flour so that the dough is not sticky. Rub the dough all over with oil, turn it into a bowl, cover and let rise until double, approximately 1 to 1-1/2 hours.

When doubled, punch the dough down and turn it out onto a *lightly oiled* bread board. Knead it again lightly, cover it with a towel again and let rest for 10 minutes. At the end of that time, cut the dough into 6 to 8 even pieces and shape each piece into a ball. Cover these balls with the towel again and let rise for 30 minutes. At the end of that time, flatten the balls with a floured rolling pin, rolling each ball into a circle 1/8-to 1/4-inch thick and 7 or 8 inches across. The circles of dough must be smooth and even; *if there are any creases in the dough the bread will not rise properly in the oven.*

Oil a cookie sheet and dust it with a little corn meal. Place the oven rack on the lowest rung and make certain that the oven is at 500° F. *This is important.* Now place 2 or 3 of the rounds on the cookie sheet and place in the oven. *Do not open the oven door for the first 5 minutes, or else the loaves will not puff and form a pocket.* Bake for a total of 8 to 10 minutes, depending on the thickness and size of the loaves. Remove to racks to cool, and continue baking until all loaves are done. The loaves will deflate on cooling.

Note. You can use less white flour and more whole wheat flour if you wish. I have on occasion used all whole wheat flour. You must keep in mind, however, whole wheat flour's extra absorbency. You may not need as much whole wheat flour by measure as you need if using all white flour. The remaining instructions stay the same.

Tender Egg Bread

Tender and delicious, this whole wheat bread also makes good cinnamon rolls or raisin bread. See Success Tips before beginning recipe.

1/2 cup lukewarm water
1-1/2 cakes yeast
1 tablespoon honey or brown
   sugar
1-1/2 cups lukewarm water
2/3 cup salad oil, melted butter,
   or margarine

1 tablespoon salt
3 tablespoons honey or brown
   sugar
4 large eggs
5 to 6 cups whole wheat or
   graham flour

Combine 1/2 cup lukewarm water, yeast and 1 tablespoon honey or sugar in a bowl and let proof. When ready, add the remaining 1-1/2 cups water, salad oil, salt, sweetening, and eggs. Stir together and then add 3 cups of the flour. Beat with a wooden spoon until smooth. Now begin adding the rest of the flour, using just enough to make a tender, medium dough. Turn the dough out onto a very lightly floured board and knead, using just enough flour to keep the dough from sticking. Remember that if you think you have used a bit too much flour, then spread the board with a thin film of oil. When you have kneaded the dough enough, spread it with a thin film of oil, turn the dough into a bowl, cover and let rise until doubled. When the dough has doubled, which takes approximately 1-1/2 to 2 hours, punch it down and turn out onto a lightly floured, or oiled, board again. You can make 1 large, lovely braided loaf (for instructions see page 126), or you can make 2 free-form loaves with the dough. Place on an oiled cookie sheet, cover and let rise until double again. Brush with an egg wash. Bake in a 350° F oven for 40 to 55 minutes, depending on whether you have made 1 or 2 loaves.

CINNAMON ROLLS. Roll the dough out into a rectangle about 1/4 to 1/2 inch thick. Spread with softened butter, and then as thickly or thinly as desired with brown sugar, some chopped nuts and raisins, and a bit of cinnamon. Roll up, sealing the edges with a little water. Cut into 1-inch slices and place, cut side down, on an oiled jelly roll pan, or in buttered muffin cups. Let rise until doubled, and then bake in a preheated 375° F oven approximately 20 minutes, or until done. Cool and glaze, if desired.

Note. Instead of sprinkling the dough with cinnamon, you can add 1 or 2 teaspoons to the dough along with the first addition of flour.

RAISIN BREAD. Increase sweetening to 1/3 cup. Add 1 or 2 teaspoons of cinnamon to the dough with the first addition of flour. Add 1/2 to 3/4 cup of raisins that have been soaked in warm water or brandy, and then drained and patted dry. If you use the brandy it is reusable. This bread is especially nice braided and then glazed when cooked.

Note. Because the bread is rich it will keep even better than most. Store in plastic bags in the refrigerator for 4 or 5 days. Frozen, it will keep for months.

Whole Wheat Cheddar Bread

An excellent quick bread, good on a snack tray.

1-1/4 cups white or unbleached white flour	1-1/4 cups whole wheat or graham flour
1/3 cup white or brown sugar	1 large egg, beaten
1 teaspoon baking powder	1-1/4 cups milk
1 teaspoon baking soda	1/4 cup melted butter or margarine or salad oil
1 teaspoon salt	1/4 cup light molasses, syrup, or honey
2 cups grated Cheddar cheese	

Sift the white flour into a bowl. Add the sugar, baking powder, soda, and salt and stir together. Stir in the grated cheese and whole wheat flour and blend together. Combine the egg, milk, oil, and molasses. Stir until blended. Add all at once to the dry ingredients and blend together gently. All of the dry ingredients should be thoroughly moistened, but the blending of ingredients must be gentle or you will end up with a coarse grain. Turn into a buttered 9-inch loaf pan or into 6 miniature loaf pans. Bake in a preheated 350° F oven for 45 minutes for a large loaf, or 35 minutes for a small loaf, or until a wire tester comes out clean. Turn out onto a rack to cool.

Cowboy Bread

This is an unusual crispy, crunchy, and very old type of bread, easily made over any campfire, or on a stove. My sons can afford the calories so they eat this bread with chili, or with any type of homemade bean soup.

1 cup whole wheat or graham flour	4 teaspoons baking powder
1 cup white flour	1 teaspoon salt
	1/2 cup water (you may need a tablespoon or so more)

Combine dry ingredients and stir them together. Add the water gradually, working mixture into a medium soft dough. Form into 2 or 3 pancake-like circles. Fry in hot fat, turning once. The bread should be crisp and lightly browned. Drain and serve at once, with plenty of butter.

Cracked Wheat Bread

This is one of the best breads I have ever tasted. It's chewy, full of flavor, and nutritious. What more can you ask for. It can be made into loaves, rolls, or long rolls. The long rolls make excellent sandwiches.

1-1/2 cups cracked wheat	3 cakes yeast dissolved in 1/3 cup lukewarm water
2 cups water	
3 cups water	1 cup wheat germ
1 cup brown sugar, or honey, or a mixture of sugar, honey and molasses	1-1/2 cups sesame seeds
	1 cup skim milk *powder*
2 tablespoons salt	9 cups flour: a mixture of rye, whole wheat (or graham), and white flours
1/4 cup salad oil, or melted margarine or lard	

Combine the cracked wheat and 2 cups water in a saucepan. Simmer for 10 minutes, or until wheat is tender and has absorbed the water. Add the remaining 3 cups water, the sugar, salt, and oil. Heat until lukewarm and pour into a large mixing bowl. Dissolve the yeast as directed and stir in. Now combine the wheat germ, sesame seeds and skim milk powder with half of the mixed flours. Stir into the liquid mixture and beat until thoroughly blended.

When the batter — for that's what it is now — is smooth, begin adding the remaining flour. Stir it in a little at a time, until a spoon can no longer stir it. Then use your hands, adding just enough of the flour to make a medium dough. Spread some of the remaining flour mixture on a clean breadboard, turn the dough onto it, and knead the dough until smooth and elastic, using more of the flour mixture as needed. Remember however, that it is better to use a little *less* flour than to use too much. Spread the dough with oil or melted margarine and place in a clean bowl. Cover and let rise until doubled. When dough has doubled, punch it down, turn out onto a *very* lightly floured board and cut into 3 pieces. Mold each piece into a loaf shape and place in buttered loaf pans. Cover again and let rise until doubled. Bake the loaves in a preheated 350° F oven for approximately 45 minutes, or until loaves test done.

TO FREEZE. See page 126.

Wheat Berry Bread

In this delicious *and* nutritious bread you can use either the wheat berries, or you can use the new hybrid grain called triticale. Triticale is a cross between wheat and rye and contains a more complete protein than either. It comes in berries, as flour, or as flakes. The flavor is somewhat like rye and like rye flour triticale doesn't contain enough gluten to provide the necessary elasticity and doesn't rise well by itself. For this reason it needs to be combined with wheat flour. Please read Success Tips before starting.

1/2 cup wheat berries, triticale
    berries or cracked wheat
boiling water to cover
2 cakes yeast
3-1/2 cups lukewarm water
1 cup skim milk crystals
1-1/2 tablespoons salt
1 tablespoon honey
1 tablespoon molasses or
    brown sugar

1/3 cup melted butter, or
    margarine or vegetable oil
1 large egg
1 tablespoon each: corn meal
    and sesame seeds
4-1/2 cups stirred and
    measured whole wheat
    flour
1 cup soy flour
1/2 cup wheat germ

3/4 cup bran

Pour the boiling water over the wheat berries and let them soak for an hour or longer.

Dissolve yeast in 1/2 cup of the lukewarm water and let sit until the yeast foams. Dissolve the milk crystals in the remaining 3 cups water and combine with the salt, honey, molasses, melted butter, egg, corn meal, sesame seeds and 2 cups of the whole wheat flour. Beat until mixture forms a smooth batter and then add the soy flour, wheat germ, bran, and softened wheat berries. Add the remaining flour, 1 cup at a time, until dough is easy to handle.

Turn dough out onto a lightly floured bread board, cover, and let the dough rest for 20 minutes. Then knead the dough until it is smooth and elastic, a good 20 minutes. For a bread of this type it is good to have an electric heavy-duty mixer to do the work for you.

When dough has been kneaded, turn it into a greased bowl and turn the dough all around so that it is greased all over. Cover and let it rise until doubled, approximately 1-1/2 hours.

When dough has risen until doubled, punch it down and let it rise again. Then punch the dough down and shape into 2 loaves. Place in greased standard 9-inch loaf pans, cover and let rise one last time until doubled in bulk, approximately 1 hour.

Brush the loaves with milk just before baking in a preheated 350° F oven for 50 minutes, or until loaves test done. Cool on racks. Makes 2 loaves.

Triticale Bread

This is a delicious, moist bread which is especially nutritious because it is made with high-protein triticale flour. Please read Success Tips before starting.

3/4 cup lukewarm water
3 cakes yeast
1 teaspoon brown sugar, honey, or molasses
1-1/2 cups lukewarm water mixed with 2/3 cup skim milk crystals
1 tablespoon salt

1/3 cup brown sugar, honey, or molasses
1/3 cup vegetable oil
4-1/2 cups stirred and measured triticale flour
2 to 3 cups stirred and measured white or unbleached white flour

Combine the 3/4 cup lukewarm water with the yeast and 1 teaspoon of brown sugar. Proof for 5 to 8 minutes. Then stir in remaining water mixed with milk crystals, the salt, brown sugar, and vegetable oil.

Stir in 2 cups each of the triticale flour and the white flour. Beat until mixture forms a smooth, very soft dough. Then add remaining flour, 1 cup at a time, until it forms a medium-soft dough.

Turn dough out onto a lightly floured bread board and knead until dough is smooth and elastic, adding more flour as necessary.

When dough has been kneaded turn it into a greased bowl, turning the dough so that it is greased all over. Cover and let rise until doubled in bulk. When dough has doubled, punch it down and divide into 2 parts. Shape each part into a loaf and place in greased 9-inch bread pans. Cover and let rise until doubled. Then bake in a preheated 375° F oven for 40 to 50 minutes, or until bread tests done. Cool on racks. Makes 2 loaves.

Whole Wheat Cream Bread

This sweetish loaf is one of our favorites, and the dough can be used as the foundation for all kinds of whole wheat coffeecakes and rolls. The heavy cream helps to make a tender dough. Please read Success Tips before beginning.

1 cup hot water
1/3 to 1/2 cup honey, brown
   sugar, or molasses
1 cup heavy cream or
   evaporated whole or
   non-fat milk

2 cakes yeast
4 large eggs
5 to 6 cups stirred and measured
   whole wheat flour

Combine hot water, honey and heavy cream. Stir to dissolve honey and let mixture cool to lukewarm. When liquid is cooled add the yeast and let it proof for 5 minutes.

When mixture is foamy, beat in 2 cups of the flour and the eggs. Add enough of the remaining flour, 1 cup at a time, to make a medium dough that can be kneaded. Turn dough out onto a lightly floured bread board and knead, adding just enough flour to keep from sticking, until dough is smooth and elastic. Turn dough into a greased bowl, turn dough so that it is greased all over, cover, and let rise until doubled in bulk.

When dough has doubled, punch it down and shape as desired into small loaves, rolls or coffeecake. Cover again and let rise until not quite doubled in bulk. Bake in a preheated 375° F oven until browned and done, about 30 minutes.

VARIATION. Dough can be rolled out and spread with plumped raisins, cinnamon, and brown sugar. Roll as for a jelly roll and cut into 1-inch slices. Place slices, cut side down, in a pan that has been greased and then spread with a mixture of honey and cream. This forms a caramel coating during the baking and is very good.

Whole Wheat Butter Dips

This was a popular quick bread during the 1960's. It has long since dropped from sight, but, made with whole wheat flour, it is certainly worth a place in the cook's recipe file. Extremely easy to make, the variations are good also. Please read Success Tips before beginning.

1/2 cup margarine or butter
2 cups whole wheat flour,
   stirred
1 teaspoon salt

1 tablespoon brown sugar
2 teaspoons baking powder
2 large eggs
1/2 to 3/4 cup milk

Put the margarine or butter in a 9-by 13-by 2-inch baking pan and place in a 425° F oven to melt.

While the butter is melting combine the dry ingredients in a mixing bowl. Stir together. Combine the eggs and milk and stir together to blend. Add all at once to the dry ingredients, and stir together until the dry ingredients are thoroughly moistened. Turn the dough out onto a floured bread board. Knead lightly, no more than 10 times, using a little more flour if needed. Now pat the dough out with your hands until it is a rectangle about 1/2 inch thick. Cut into strips. Carefully pick up each strip and dip both sides in the melted butter in the pan. Lay the strips close together in the pan. Bake for 15 to 20 minutes, or until done.

VARIATIONS. You can add 1/2 cup shredded sharp Cheddar cheese to the dry ingredients. Or you can sprinkle garlic powder into the melted butter. Or add 1/4 to 1/3 cup minced parsley or chives to the dough.

Wheat Germ Rolls

If you use the larger amount of sugar in this recipe, it will be sweet enough to use for cinnamon or orange rolls. With the lesser amount of sweetening, the recipe makes a good dinner roll. *I occasionally substitute 1 cup rice polish, rye, buckwheat or soy flour for the same amount of whole wheat flour.* Please read Success Tips before beginning.

1/2 cup lukewarm water	1/4 to 3/4 cup brown sugar,
2 cakes yeast	honey or molasses
1 teaspoon brown sugar,	2 large eggs
honey or molasses	4 cups stirred and measured
1-1/2 cups lukewarm water	whole wheat flour
mixed with 2/3 cup skim	1 cup wheat germ
milk crystals	1 tablespoon salt

Combine the 1/2 cup lukewarm water with yeast and the teaspoon of brown sugar. Let proof for 5 minutes. Then stir in the remaining lukewarm water, brown sugar, eggs and 3 cups of the flour. Beat until thoroughly mixed. If you have a heavy-duty mixer, beat the dough for 5 to 10 minutes.

When dough has been thoroughly beaten, stir in the wheat germ, salt, and enough more flour to make a firm dough. Grease the dough all over, cover with a towel, and let the dough rise until doubled in bulk, approximately 45 minutes to an hour.

When dough has doubled, punch it down and let it rise again.

When dough has risen the second time, punch it down and turn out onto a lightly floured bread board. Knead lightly and shape into rolls. Place in greased pans, cover and let rise until almost, but not quite doubled. Bake in a preheated 375° F oven until browned and done, about 20 minutes. Makes approximately 24 rolls.

Refrigerator Whole Wheat Rolls

A convenience for the cook who doesn't have time to bake from scratch each time, but still prefers homemade to store-bought. Please read Success Tips before beginning.

1-1/2 cups hot water	1/2 cup lukewarm water
1/2 cup brown sugar or honey	1/2 cup skim milk *powder*
1 tablespoon salt	4 to 4-1/2 cups whole wheat or
1/4 cup salad oil or melted	graham flour
margarine or lard	3 large eggs, beaten
2 cakes yeast	3 cups white flour

Pour the hot water over the sugar, salt, and oil. Stir until sugar and salt are dissolved. Let cool. Dissolve the yeast in the 1/2 cup lukewarm water. Let stand until foamy then add to the sugar mixture. Stir the skim milk powder into the whole wheat flour. Beat this into the sugar mixture along with the eggs. Beat all together. Now begin adding the white flour, a little at a time, using just enough to make a medium dough. Mix together thoroughly as this will eliminate any need for kneading. Spread all over with oil, place in a bowl, cover, and refrigerate. The dough will keep for approximately 4 days. Punch it down at least once a day.

When ready to use, remove the required amount of dough from the refrigerator 2 hours before you wish to serve the rolls. Turn the dough onto a *very* lightly floured, or oiled, bread board and knead a few times. Shape as desired and place on oiled cookie sheets, or in oiled pans. Cover and let rise until doubled, about 1 to 1-1/2 hours. Bake in a preheated 400° F oven for 15 to 20 minutes, or until done.

Brush with melted butter as soon as you remove the rolls from the oven.

bread— 25 min. at 425 in preheated pan.

Whole Wheat Corn Meal Muffins

These delicious little muffins are better than cake. They're nutritious, delicious, and, if you are pressed for time, the batter can be made up to 24 hours ahead and refrigerated until needed. The batter will loosen a little and will be thinner than if it is baked immediately, but there will be no harm to the flavor. Please read Success Tips before starting.

2 cups stone-ground yellow corn meal	2 tablespoons baking powder
1-1/4 cups whole wheat or graham flour, stirred	1-1/2 teaspoons salt
1 cup soy flour	2 cups milk
1/4 cup wheat germ	1 cup corn or safflower oil
	1/2 cup honey
	1/2 cup brown sugar, packed
4 large eggs	

Combine dry ingredients in a large bowl and stir together. Combine liquid ingredients, brown sugar, and eggs in a smaller bowl and beat together lightly. Stir into the dry ingredients remembering that a muffin batter should be mixed *just until* the dry ingredients are thoroughly moistened. If you beat the batter you will ruin it. Bake immediately, or refrigerate as suggested above. To bake, pour into greased muffin tins, filling them just 3/4 full. Bake for 15 to 20 minutes in a preheated 400° F oven. Remove from pans to cool. Makes between 2 and 2-1/2 dozen muffins.

Raised Whole Wheat Biscuits

Serve these hot from the oven, or split and toasted. They are excellent with breakfast or a salad or soup lunch. See Success Tips before starting.

2 cakes yeast	1/2 cup honey, molasses, or brown sugar
2 cups lukewarm water	1 tablespoon salt
1/2 cup salad oil, or melted margarine, butter, or lard	1/3 to 1/2 cup sesame seeds
1/3 cup wheat germ	
4 to 5 cups whole wheat or graham flour	

Dissolve the yeast in the water. Then stir in the oil, sweetening, salt, sesame seeds, wheat germ, and 2 cups of the flour. Beat with a wooden spoon. Now gradually beat in as much of the remaining flour as the mixture will hold. It should be a medium dough. Turn out onto a very lightly floured bread board. If you think that you may have added a bit *too* much flour, and the dough feels a little stiff, then use a little oil instead of flour on the bread board. Either way, knead the dough until smooth and elastic, about 5 to 8 minutes. Brush dough all over with oil, turn into a bowl, cover and let rise until doubled. This will take about 1-1/2 to 2 hours.

When dough has doubled, punch it down, turn out onto an oiled board, and roll out to a thickness of approximately 1/2 inch. Cut with a floured biscuit cutter, or a floured glass. Place on oiled cookie sheets, cover and let rise again for 45 minutes to an hour. Then bake in a preheated 375° F oven for 20 minutes, or until browned and done. Makes 2 to 3 dozen depending on the size cutter you use.

Whole Wheat Brown and Serve Rolls

You can use just about any favorite bread or roll dough to make brown and serve rolls since it is the technique that is standard, not the recipe. Please read Success Tips before beginning.

1/2 cup lukewarm water	1 large egg, beaten
2 cakes yeast	1 tablespoon salt
1/4 cup brown sugar, honey, or	2-1/2 cups lukewarm water
molasses	6 to 7 cups stirred and measured
1/4 cup vegetable oil	whole wheat flour
1 cup wheat germ	

Combine 1/2 cup lukewarm water with yeast and brown sugar. Proof for 5 minutes. Then add oil, egg, salt and remaining water. Stir in 3 cups of the flour and beat until mixture forms a smooth batter.

Beat in 1 more cup of the flour and the wheat germ, beating thoroughly. Now add just enough of the remaining flour to form a medium dough. Turn out onto a lightly floured bread board and knead until it is smooth and elastic, adding just enough flour as needed to keep the dough from sticking.

Turn dough into a greased bowl, and turn the dough so that it is greased all over. Cover and let rise until doubled in bulk, approximately 1 hour.

When dough has doubled, punch it down and turn out onto a lightly floured surface again. Shape as desired, or place in greased muffin tins. Cover and let rise until not quite doubled, about 3/4 in bulk.

Bake in a preheated 275° F oven for 40 minutes, or until done in the middle, but not yet browned. Remove from the oven and let cool in the tins for 20 minutes. Then remove rolls from the tins and finish cooling. Wrap and store in the freezer for up to 2 months, or in the refrigerator for up to 2 weeks. To complete baking, take directly from refrigerator or freezer and place in a preheated 400° F oven to bake just until browned, about 8 to 10 minutes. Makes 4 dozen rolls.

Mixed Grain
Breads

STURDY, delicious breads, full of flavor and extremely nutritious, can be made from a variety of grains. When I was first experimenting with making my own breads, and branching out from the traditional white or whole wheat breads, I used to go to the health food store and buy small amounts of assorted flours and grains. I made breads using bran and bran flour, rolled oats and oat flour, rye flour and meal, brown rice flour, soy flour, sesame meal, sunflower seed meal, rice polish, wheat germ, and just about anything else that looked interesting or nutritious. Some I never used again in breads, not liking either the flavor or the texture, but many I have continued to use. Soy flour, wheat germ, rye flour and meal, bran, and rolled oats are always in my freezer. I especially like the flavor of the newer triticale flour, and use it often.

I've included recipes for the mixed grain breads that have withstood the test of time in my own household, and for a few others that are tasty enough to make at least occasionally. And of course there are some, like pumpernickel, that are always popular.

Success Tips for Mixed Grain Breads

1.   Try to buy your various flours and meals in a health food store. The flours will not contain preservatives and will have much more flavor than those bought in regular markets.

2.   Store the flours and meals in a refrigerator, or, better yet, in the freezer. With freezer storage, the flours and meals will remain stable for years. If refrigerated, they will still keep for at least several months, depending on the temperature of the refrigerator. But kept at room temperature, good flours and meals will become rancid within a short time. The increase in flavor and nutrition is well worth whatever inconvenience there may be.

3.   If you are experimenting with flours and meals that you are not used to, begin by adding small amounts to the recipe you are using. Especially with such items as sunflower seed meal, sesame seed meal or millet meal, I wouldn't recommend using more than 1/2 to 1 cup in a recipe. Try rye meal as a substitute for a cup of flour in a rye bread recipe.

4.   Remember that breads using the whole grains and meals are heavier than breads without them. This means that the rising time for the dough will be longer, so remember to make allowances.

5.   If you want you can replace 1/2 cup, or more, of the flour in any of the recipes in this chapter with the same amount of whole wheat flour, oat flour, brown rice flour, sunflower meal, bran flakes, wheat germ, rye flour, buckwheat flour or corn meal. I would recommend using a small amount until you are certain that you enjoy the difference in taste and texture.

Mixed Grain Bread I

This sturdy bread has a nutty and delicious flavor. *If you want you can use rolled oats in place of the oat flour. However, oat flour is easily made in the food processor from rolled oats, and gives a slightly different flavor and texture.* Please read Success Tips before beginning.

1-1/2 cups steel cut oats
3 cups water
1/3 cup butter or margarine
2 cakes yeast
1 cup lukewarm water
1/4 cup brown sugar

1 tablespoon salt
1 cup rolled oats or oat flour
1 cup corn meal
2 cups stirred and measured
   whole wheat flour
3/4 cup lukewarm water,
   approximately

Soak the steel cut oats in the 3 cups water overnight. In the morning cook them in a double boiler, over hot water, until they are softened. Take 1-1/2 cups of the cereal mixture and pour it into a large mixing bowl. Add the butter and stir to melt it. Cool to lukewarm and then add the yeast which has been dissolved in the 1 cup lukewarm water. Now stir in the sugar, salt, rolled oats, corn meal and flour. Add just enough of the remaining water to make a workable dough. This will be a heavy dough, and shouldn't be too moist. Work the dough a few minutes. Then rub it all over with oil, cover and let rise until doubled in bulk. Punch the dough down and let it rise another hour. When dough has risen the second time, punch it down and turn into a well-greased 9-inch loaf pan. Cover and let rise again until light, and bake in a preheated 375° F oven for 1 hour to an hour and 10 minutes.

    Note. If there is too much dough for a standard sized loaf pan, use two 8-inch loaf pans, or make 1 loaf and some rolls.

Mixed Grain Bread II

This makes a dense, heavy loaf that is tasty, chewy and good for you. It's marvelous when toasted. Please read Success Tips before beginning.

2-3/4 cups boiling water
1 cup bran flakes
1 cup old-fashioned rolled oats
1/3 cup vegetable oil
2 teaspoons salt
1 cup raisins
2 cakes yeast

1/2 cup lukewarm water
3/4 cup mild flavored honey
1-1/2 cups wheat germ
3 cups stirred and measured
   whole wheat flour
2-1/2 to 3 cups stirred and
   measured unbleached
   white or white flour

Combine the boiling water, bran flakes, rolled oats, vegetable oil, salt and raisins in a large bowl. Stir to mix and set aside until cooled to lukewarm. Dissolve the yeast in the 1/2 cup lukewarm water and then add to the cooled mixture.

Stir in the honey, wheat germ and whole wheat flour. Then add the white flour a cup at a time, mixing it in until you have a dough that is medium firm. Turn out onto a lightly floured bread board and knead until smooth and elastic.

When dough has been kneaded enough turn it into a greased bowl, turn the dough around so that it is covered with grease on all surfaces, cover with a clean towel and let rise until doubled in bulk. This will take approximately 1 hour. When dough has risen, punch it down and place in 2 greased bread pans. Cover and let rise until doubled again. Then bake in a preheated 350° F oven for 50 to 55 minutes, or until loaves test done. Makes 2 loaves.

Six Grain Bread

This makes a very good, flavorful bread. If you want you might substitute 1/2 cup of buckwheat flour for the same amount of white flour, or for some other flour that you might not have. Remember that bread recipes are flexible. If you don't have the soy, or the whole wheat, or the rye, substitute another flour that you do have. Maybe corn flour, or corn meal. Or buckwheat flour, or brown rice flour. Please read Success Tips before beginning.

2 cups rolled oats, or rye or wheat flakes	1/2 cup wheat germ
	1/2 cup soy flour
2 tablespoons butter or margarine or vegetable oil	1/2 cup whole wheat flour
	1/2 cup rye flour
1/2 cup honey, brown sugar, or molasses, or a mixture	1 cake yeast dissolved in 1/4 cup lukewarm water
2 teaspoons salt	3 cups stirred and measured
2 cups very hot water	white or unbleached white
1-1/2 cups skim milk powder	flour

Combine the rolled oats, butter, honey and salt in a mixing bowl. Pour the very hot water over the mixture and stir to mix thoroughly. Stir the skim milk powder, wheat germ, soy flour, whole wheat and rye flours together. Add the proofed yeast and skim milk powder mixture to the cooled oat mixture. Mix thoroughly and then add the white flour, 1 cup at a time, until you have a medium dough.

Turn the dough out onto a lightly floured surface and knead until elastic. Then turn into an oiled bowl and oil the surface of the dough. Cover and let rise until doubled in bulk, about 1 to 1-1/2 hours.

When dough has doubled in bulk, punch it down and divide into 2 parts. Shape into loaves and place in greased 9-inch loaf pans. Cover and let rise until doubled in bulk again. Bake in a preheated 350° F oven for 45 to 55 minutes, or until loaves test done.

Makes 2 loaves.

High Protein Bread

The soy flour increases the protein value of this bread and adds a nutty flavor of its own. The addition of the wheat germ makes this about as healthful a bread as you could possibly make. Please read Success Tips before beginning.

2 cakes yeast	1 cup wheat germ
2-1/4 cups lukewarm water	1-1/2 cups soy flour
2 large eggs	2 tablespoons brown sugar or
1/2 cup vegetable oil	honey or molasses
3-1/2 cups stirred and	1 tablespoon salt
measured white or	3/4 cup skim milk powder
unbleached white flour	

Combine yeast and water in electric mixer bowl. Let proof for 5 minutes. Add the eggs and oil and 2 cups of the white flour. Mix well and then stir together the remaining ingredients and add to the bowl, beating all the while. Beat until the dough leaves the sides of the bowl.

Remove dough to a lightly floured surface and knead until smooth and elastic. Cover the dough and let it rest for 20 minutes. Then shape the dough into 2 loaves to fit 8-inch greased loaf pans. Cover and let rise until doubled in bulk and then bake in a preheated 375° F oven for 40 to 45 minutes, or until loaves are browned and done. Makes 2 loaves.

Oat Bran Bread

This bread is excellent toasted. Please read Success Tips before beginning.

1 cup bran flakes	3/4 cup honey or brown sugar
1 cup rolled oats	or molasses
1 tablespoon salt	1-1/2 cups wheat germ
1 cup raisins	3 cups stirred and measured
1/3 cup vegetable oil	whole wheat flour
2-3/4 cups boiling water	2-1/2 cups stirred and
2 cakes yeast	measured white or
1/2 cup lukewarm water	unbleached white flour

Combine the bran, oats, salt, raisins, oil and boiling water. Stir to mix thoroughly. Dissolve the yeast in the lukewarm water. Let it proof for 5 minutes and while it is proofing stir the honey into the boiling water mixture. Cool to lukewarm and then add the yeast and wheat germ and the whole wheat flour. Beat thoroughly. And then stir in enough of the white flour to make a medium firm dough.

Turn the dough out onto a lightly floured surface and knead for 5 to 8 minutes, or until elastic. Turn into an oiled bowl and turn the dough so that it is oiled all over. Cover and let rise until doubled, about 1 hour. When doubled, punch the dough down and divide into 2 parts. Shape into loaves and place in greased 9-inch loaf pans. Cover and let rise again until doubled in bulk. Bake in a preheated 350° F oven for 50 to 55 minutes, or until loaves test done.

Makes 2 loaves.

Rolled Oats Bread

For this moist bread you can use either rolled oats or rolled rye or wheat flakes. The rye or wheat flakes can be substituted for the rolled oats in other recipes also. Please read Success Tips before beginning.

1/4 cup vegetable oil
1/3 cup honey, molasses or
    maple syrup
1 tablespoon salt
3/4 cup skim milk powder
1-3/4 cups very hot water
2 cakes yeast dissolved in
    1/2 cup lukewarm water

3 cups stirred and measured
    white or unbleached white
    flour
1 cup wheat germ
1-1/4 cups rolled oats
    (see above)
2-1/2 cups stirred and
    measured whole wheat
    flour

Combine the oil, honey, salt and milk powder in a large mixing bowl. Pour the hot water over and beat until smooth. Cool to lukewarm and add the yeast which has been proofed in the lukewarm water.

Now add 2 cups of the white flour and beat until smooth. Add the wheat germ, rolled oats and whole wheat flour and mix well. If the dough is too sticky add enough of the remaining cup of white flour to make a fairly non-sticky dough. Remember that you will be adding more flour when you knead the dough, so don't add too much now.

Turn the dough out onto lightly floured surface and knead until elastic, about 8 minutes.

Turn the dough into a clean, oiled bowl and rub the surface of the dough with oil. Cover and let rise until doubled in bulk, about 1 hour. When doubled, punch the dough down and divide into 2 parts. Shape into loaves and place in buttered 9-inch loaf pans. Cover and let rise until doubled in bulk again. Bake the loaves in a preheated 350° F oven for 50 minutes, or until the loaves test done.

Makes 2 loaves.

Basic Rye Bread

This is a good *basic* rye bread recipe. You might vary it by using 1 cup of scalded, cooled milk in place of the same amount of water. And of course you might use whole wheat flour in place of part of the white flour. Or substitute 1/2 cup of wheat germ or bran flakes for 1/2 cup of flour. Please read Success Tips before beginning.

4 to 4-1/2 cups stirred and
    measured white or
    unbleached white flour
2 packages active dry yeast

2 cups lukewarm water
1/2 cup brown sugar, honey
    or molasses
2 teaspoons salt

2 cups rye meal or flour

This bread is made by the RapidMix method. In a large electric mixer bowl combine 3 cups of the white flour with the yeast. Stir together. Combine the water, honey, salt, and rye meal. Add to the flour mixture and beat at low speed, scraping the sides of the bowl frequently. Then beat at high speed for a minute. Remove bowl from mixer and add enough of the remaining white flour to make a firm dough.

Turn dough out onto a lightly floured surface and knead until smooth and elastic. Turn dough into a clean, oiled bowl and turn the dough so that it is covered with a film of oil. Cover the bowl and let rise until doubled in bulk. *At this point the dough could be refrigerated overnight if desired.* When ready to bake, punch the dough down and divide into 2 parts. Shape into loaves and place in greased 8-inch loaf pans. Cover and let rise until almost, but not quite, doubled. Bake in a preheated 375° F oven for 40 to 45 minutes, or until loaves test done.

Note. For a professional touch, you might make a glaze by beating 1 egg yolk with 1 tablespoon water and brush the loaves with this right before baking, and at least once during baking.

Rye Meal Bread

This bread has a fine, hearty flavor and texture. Serve it with a light meal. Please read Success Tips before beginning.

1 cup rye meal	1 tablespoon salt
1-1/2 cups water	2 cakes yeast dissolved in
1/4 cup butter or margarine	1/3 cup lukewarm water
1/3 cup honey or molasses	1 cup whole wheat flour, stirred
1 tablespoon anise seed or	and measured
caraway seed	1 cup rye flour, stirred and
	measured

Combine the rye meal and the water and soak for several hours or overnight. Then turn into the top part of a double boiler and cook over simmering water for 40 minutes. As soon as it has cooked and before it cools, turn the mixture into a large mixing bowl and add the butter, honey, seeds, and salt. Stir together and cool to lukewarm. Then add the dissolved yeast and the flours. Beat thoroughly for 2 or 3 minutes. This can be done in an electric mixer if desired. Then rub with oil, cover with a towel, and let the dough rise for an hour. When it is light, punch it down and turn into a greased 8- or 9-inch loaf pan. Cover and let rise again for 45 minutes. Put the loaf into a *cold* oven and set the heat at 400° F. Bake for 30 minutes and then reduce the heat to 300° F. Bake for 30 minutes longer. Let sit overnight, or for at least 8 hours, before cutting.

Dark Rye Bread (Pumpernickel)

In some areas of the country you can buy different grades of rye flour — the dark rye flour, the medium, and the light. If possible, obtain the dark rye flour. If not, use what is available. This is a hearty bread, fine with a good mustard and sausage. Please read Success Tips before beginning. This bread uses the RapidMix method of combining the yeast with the flour.

4-1/2 cups stirred and measured white or unbleached white flour	1 package active dry yeast
	1-3/4 cups water
	1/4 cup dark molasses
1-1/2 cups stirred and measured rye flour (see above)	1 square unsweetened chocolate (1 ounce)
4 teaspoons salt	1 tablespoon butter, margarine, or vegetable oil
1/2 cup bran flakes	1 cup mashed potatoes at room temperature
1/2 cup corn meal	
1 tablespoon caraway seeds	

Combine the white and the rye flour. Remove 2 cups of the mixture and combine with the salt, bran, 1/3 cup of the corn meal, and the yeast in electric mixer bowl. Stir thoroughly.

Combine the water, molasses, chocolate and butter in a small saucepan and heat until butter and chocolate are almost melted. Remove from heat and slowly add to the flour-yeast mixture, beating thoroughly. Now add the mashed potatoes, caraway seeds and 1-1/2 cups of the reserved white flour-rye mixture, beating thoroughly. Then add enough of the remaining flour mixture to make a soft dough. Turn the dough out onto a lightly floured surface and let it rest for 10 minutes. Then knead, adding as much flour as is necessary to make a smooth, workable dough.

When dough is kneaded, turn it into a clean, oiled bowl and oil the surface of the dough. Cover and let rise until doubled in bulk, about 1 to 1-1/2 hours. Then punch the dough down and let it rise another 30 minutes. Divide into 2 parts and shape into loaves.

The loaves can be baked on a greased and corn meal-sprinkled (use the remaining 2 tablespoons corn meal) cookie sheet, or in 2 greased 9-inch loaf pans. If you use the cookie sheet, shape the loaves into rounds or oblongs. The dough should rise for an hour before baking.

Brush loaves with a beaten egg and bake in a preheated 350°F oven for 50 minutes, or until loaves test done. Makes 2 loaves.

SOURDOUGH DARK RYE. To make a delicious sourdough rye bread simply stir 1-1/2 cups of any sourdough starter into the dry flour-yeast mixture along with the other liquid ingredients. Proceed as directed. You may need a little more flour to make a medium dough. Knead, shape, and bake loaves as directed above.

Russian Black Bread

This is the perfect bread for those who occasionally like a dark, dark, heavy bread. It goes especially well, thinly sliced, with a good mustard, cheese and sausage. Please read Success Tips before beginning. This is another recipe using the RapidMix method of combining the yeast with the flour.

4 cups stirred and measured rye flour
3 cups stirred and measured white or unbleached white flour
1 tablespoon salt
1 teaspoon sugar
2 cups bran flakes
2 tablespoons caraway seeds
2 teaspoons instant coffee powder (not freeze-dried)

2 teaspoons onion powder
2 packages active dry yeast
2-1/2 cups water
1/4 cup vinegar
1/4 cup dark molasses
1 square unsweetened chocolate (1 ounce)
1/4 cup butter or margarine or vegetable oil
Glaze: 1 teaspoon cornstarch cooked with 1/2 cup water

Combine rye and white flour. Turn 2-1/3 cups of flour mixture into the large bowl of an electric mixer with the salt, sugar, bran flakes, caraway seeds, coffee, onion powder and yeast. Stir to mix.

Combine water, vinegar, molasses, chocolate and butter in a saucepan and heat until quite warm. Slowly add to the dry ingredients beating with the electric mixer for 2 minutes at medium speed. Scrape the bowl occasionally. Then add enough of the remaining flour mixture to make a soft dough. Turn this dough out onto a lightly floured surface and let it rest for 10 minutes. Then knead the dough. The dough will remain slightly sticky.

When kneaded, turn the dough into a clean, oiled bowl and oil the surface of the dough. Cover and let rise until doubled in bulk, about 1 to 1-1/2 hours. Punch the dough down and turn out onto a lightly floured surface again. Divide into 2 parts and shape each part into a round loaf. Place in greased and corn meal-sprinkled 8-inch round cake pans. Cover and let rise again until doubled, about 1 hour.

Bake in a preheated 350° F oven for 45 to 55 minutes, or until loaves test done. Brush with cornstarch glaze and return bread to oven for 2 or 3 minutes, or until glaze is set. Remove from pans and cool on racks.

Makes 2 loaves.

Granola Soy Bread

This sweet bread packs an extra nutritional punch, with both wheat germ and soy flour. Children love it. Please read Success Tips before beginning.

2 cups hot water
2 tablespoons butter,
   margarine or vegetable oil
1/4 cup honey or molasses or
   brown sugar
1/2 cup orange marmalade
1 cup granola (preferably
   homemade)

2 cups stirred and measured
   whole wheat flour
1/2 cup wheat germ
1 tablespoon salt
1/2 cup soy flour
2 packages active dry yeast
3-1/2 cups stirred and
   measured white or
   unbleached white flour

Combine hot water with butter, honey and marmalade in a saucepan. Heat until butter is melted. Cool to lukewarm. In the large bowl of an electric mixer combine the granola, whole wheat flour, wheat germ, salt, soy flour, and the yeast. Stir together with 1 cup of the white flour. Now pour the warm liquid mixture over the flour mixture and beat at medium speed for 3 minutes. Don't forget to scrape the sides of the bowl. Then add enough of the remaining white flour, 1 cup at a time, to make a medium firm dough.

Turn the dough out onto a lightly floured surface and knead, adding a little more flour if necessary to make a non-sticky dough. Turn the dough into a clean, oiled bowl and oil the surface of the dough. Cover and let rise until doubled in bulk, about 1 hour. When the dough has doubled, punch it down and divide into 2 parts. Shape into loaves and place in 2 greased 9-inch bread pans. Cover and let rise again until doubled. Bake in a preheated 375° F oven for 40 minutes, or until loaves test done.

Makes 2 loaves.

Cracked Wheat Oatmeal Bread

This fine bread makes exceptional toast. Please read Success Tips before beginning.

1 cup rolled oats	1 cup plain yogurt or sour cream
1 cup cracked wheat	1/4 cup vegetable oil
1 cup boiling water	1 tablespoon salt
2 cakes yeast dissolved in	1 cup wheat germ
1/2 cup lukewarm water	4 cups stirred and measured
1 tablespoon honey or brown	white or unbleached white
sugar or molasses	flour

Combine rolled oats and cracked wheat and pour boiling water over them. Cool to lukewarm. Proof yeast and stir into the cooled rolled oat mixture along with the honey, yogurt, oil, and salt. Stir together. Beat in the wheat germ and 2 cups of the flour. Gradually add remaining flour, 1 cup at a time, until you have a firm dough. Turn the dough out onto a lightly floured surface and knead until elastic, adding a little flour as needed to keep the dough from sticking. Turn dough into an oiled bowl, and rub the surface of the dough with oil. Cover and let rise until doubled in bulk.

When doubled, punch dough down and shape into 2 loaves. Place in greased 9-inch loaf pans, cover and let rise again until doubled, about 45 minutes. Brush tops with lightly beaten egg and bake in a preheated 375° F oven for 45 to 50 minutes, or until loaves test done.

Makes 2 loaves.

Buckwheat Bread

This bread will be a favorite with buckwheat fans. Please read Success Tips before beginning.

2 cakes yeast dissolved in
  2 cups lukewarm water
1/3 cup honey, molasses or
  brown sugar
1/2 cup wheat germ
1-1/2 cups stirred and
  measured buckwheat flour

3 cups stirred and measured
  whole wheat or graham
  flour
2 tablespoons vegetable oil

Proof the yeast in the water and then stir in the honey, whole wheat flour and oil. Beat with an electric mixer or by hand until mixture forms a thick batter. Then stir in the wheat germ and buckwheat flour. Do not knead. Rub the surface of the dough with oil, cover, and let rise until doubled in bulk, about 45 minutes to an hour. Stir the dough down and transfer to a greased 9- by 5- by 3-inch loaf pan. Brush the surface of the dough with oil again, cover and let rise again until doubled in bulk. Bake in a preheated 375° F oven for 50 to 60 minutes, or until bread tests done. Cool on rack.

Makes 1 loaf.

Bran-Wheat Germ Refrigerator Rolls

Prepare this dough when you have a few free moments and store it in the refrigerator. The dough will keep for up to a week and can be baked as needed. Please read Success Tips before beginning.

1 cup butter or margarine
1/2 cup brown sugar or honey
  or molasses
2 teaspoons salt
2 cups bran flakes
1-3/4 cups boiling water
2 cakes yeast

1/2 cup lukewarm water
2 large eggs, beaten
1 cup wheat germ
5 cups stirred and measured
  white or unbleached white
  flour (up to 2-1/2 cups
  whole wheat flour may be
  used if desired)

Combine butter, sugar, salt and bran flakes in a large mixing bowl. Add boiling water and stir to melt the butter. Cool to lukewarm and then add the yeast which has been dissolved in the 1/2 cup lukewarm water. Add the eggs and the wheat germ and beat to blend. Add 2-1/2 cups of the flour and stir until smooth. Add remaining flour, 1 cup at a time, and mix in thoroughly.

When the dough has been mixed, cover the bowl tightly and refrigerate until needed. When ready to use, remove dough from refrigerator and punch it down. Flour your hands and take off pieces of dough to fill greased muffin cups about half full. Cover and let rise until doubled. Since the dough has been refrigerated this will take around 2 hours. Bake in a preheated 425° F oven for 15 minutes, or until rolls are browned and done. Total recipe makes about 36 rolls.

Oatmeal Refrigerator Rolls

The dough for these rolls will keep in the refrigerator for 3 or 4 days. When my children were younger I used to double or triple this recipe. Now it cuts down on my work when I'm catering or planning ahead for a company luncheon or dinner. Please read Success Tips before beginning.

1/2 cup butter or margarine	1 cake yeast
1/2 cup boiling water	1/2 cup lukewarm water
3 tablespoons sugar, brown	1 large egg
sugar, honey, or molasses	2-1/2 cups stirred and measured
1-1/2 teaspoons salt	white or unbleached white
1 cup old-fashioned rolled oats	flour

Combine butter, boiling water, sugar, salt, and oats. Stir to blend and cool to lukewarm. Combine yeast with the 1/2 cup lukewarm water and let proof for 5 minutes. Add to cooled oat mixture along with the egg and beat well. Add enough of the flour to make a soft dough and mix well.

Cover the pan of dough and chill in the refrigerator for several hours, or up to 3 or 4 days. When ready, form the dough into small balls and place in greased muffin tins. Cover and let rise until doubled, about 2 hours. Bake in a preheated 400° F oven until browned and done, about 20 minutes. Makes approximately 24 rolls.

Mixed Grain Biscuits

These flaky biscuits are a delicious change from the traditional. Please read Success Tips before beginning.

1 cup stirred and measured white or unbleached white flour
1/3 cup stirred and measured rye, buckwheat, or triticale flour
1/4 cup corn meal
1 tablespoon baking powder
1/2 teaspoon salt
1/2 teaspoon sugar
1 teaspoon caraway, poppy, or sesame seed
1/3 cup butter or margarine
2/3 cup milk
corn meal for dusting cookie sheet

Stir all of the dry ingredients together in a mixing bowl. Cut in the butter until mixture resembles coarse crumbs. Make a well in the center and add the milk. Stir quickly with a fork until mixture is just barely mixed. Turn out onto a very lightly floured surface and knead for no more than 10 or 12 gentle strokes. Roll or pat the dough to a thickness of 1/2 inch. Cut with a floured biscuit cutter. Place on greased and corn meal-sprinkled cookie sheet and sprinkle the tops of the biscuits with a little more corn meal. Bake in a preheated 450° F oven for 12 to 15 minutes, or until done. Makes 8 biscuits.

Rye Muffins

These excellent muffins are unusual in that they are not sweet. They make a good dinner muffin and are equally good with a soup and salad luncheon. Please read Success Tips before you begin.

2 cups stirred and measured rye flour
2 tablespoons sugar
1 tablespoon baking powder
1/2 teaspoon salt
2 large eggs, beaten
1 cup milk
1/4 cup butter, melted, or 1/4 cup vegetable oil
1/2 pound grated Swiss or Cheddar cheese

Combine the dry ingredients and stir together thoroughly. Blend eggs and milk in a mixing bowl and gradually add the dry ingredients. Stir in the butter. Using half of the batter spoon it into 24 greased muffin tins. Sprinkle the tops of each muffin with the grated cheese and cover with the remaining batter. Bake in a preheated 400° F oven for 10 minutes. Reduce heat to 350° F and continue baking for another 10 to 15 minutes. Serve hot. Makes 24 muffins.

Whey Cookery

IN a return to the more natural foods and their more basic types of cookery, many good cooks are experimenting with making their own cheeses. Whey, the milky liquid which separates from the milk when curds form, is usually thrown out, as it is highly perishable. However, whey is highly usable and can replace the water in almost any baking recipe for a more tender, richer-tasting final product. It is a flavor carrier in gravies, breads, rolls, cakes and cookies.

The dried whey is especially useful and can be used in virtually all baked products. Whey is over 70% pure milk sugar and thus can completely replace sugar in bread, rolls, biscuits, hotcakes, etc. Using it does lengthen the proofing time rather substantially, so it is recommended that you either proof to volume rather than time, or else add a small amount of regular sugar to speed the process up. However, it is simple to adjust your baking schedule to allow more time.

Success Tips and Reminders on the Use of Whey

1. Fresh, sweet, liquid whey can be used as the liquid requirement in your baking recipes. However, since some wheys are too acid and can carry undesirable flavors into the baking, it is recommended that you use the dried whey powder.

2. Whey powder does lengthen the proofing time in yeast-raised bread rather substantially. It is recommended that you use a small amount of sugar. If you are adapting a recipe to the use of whey powder and it calls for white sugar, use 2 parts of whey powder to 1 part sugar as a substitute. For example, in a recipe calling for 1 cup white sugar, change this to 2/3 cup whey powder and 1/3 cup sugar. If the recipe called for 3/4 cup sugar, you would use 1/2 cup whey powder and 1/4 cup sugar.

3. If the recipe calls for *both* brown and white sugar, use the same amount of brown sugar, and replace the white sugar with whey powder. For example, in a recipe calling for 1/2 cup *each* brown and white sugar you would use 1/2 cup brown sugar and 1/2 cup whey powder.

4. The use of whey powder increases the speed of browning. So it is recommended that you set the oven rack in the middle or the upper half of the oven, so that the baked goods do not overbrown.

5. For the same reason it is recommended that you set your oven no higher than 350° F or 375° F. Rolls which are usually baked at 400° F or 425° F will bake beautifully at 375° F.

6. The use of a blender or a small hand shaker will assure a no-lump blending of the whey powder and liquid.

7. The whey powder can also be sifted with the dry ingredients. However, since I do not recommend sifting the flour for breads, I find it much more convenient to mix the whey with the liquid.

8. Baked goods made with whey powder become stale less quickly, and have a longer shelf life.

9. Breads using whey powder will rise faster and achieve a greater volume if you will use a small amount of lecithin in the dough. The usual amount is 1/4 teaspoon for each loaf. You can use either the liquid or the granular lecithin. Simply mix it in with the warm liquid.

10. As for all bread recipes, for this one I recommend stirring the flour rather than sifting it. Stir it with a spoon, spoon it into a cup

measure, lightly so that it doesn't pack down, and level it off with a knife.

Basic Whey Bread

I've adapted the following recipe from the Forman and Weeks book *Whey Cookery,* published by Hawkes Publishing Co. in Salt Lake City. It makes a sturdy, tasty bread. The original recipe called for baking the loaves in 2 pans; however, if you use a standard bread pan, 9- by 5- by 3-inches, the dough will make one nice loaf. Please read Success Tips before beginning.

3/4 cup dried whey powder	1/3 cup vegetable oil
1-1/2 cups lukewarm water	1 tablespoon salt
2 cakes yeast	5-1/2 to 6 cups white or
1/2 cup lukewarm water	unbleached white
	flour

Blend the dried whey with the 1-1/2 cups lukewarm water. Dissolve the yeast in the 1/2 cup lukewarm water. Turn these ingredients into a mixer bowl (at least 3-quart size) and add the vegetable oil, salt and 2 cups of the flour. Beat with an electric mixer for at least 3 minutes. Gradually add the remaining flour and continue beating, using just enough flour to make a dough that is still soft, but not sticky. This bread does not need to be kneaded, nor does it require a first rising. So as soon as the dough is ready, turn it out onto a very lightly floured bread board and shape it into a loaf. Place in a greased loaf pan, cover and let rise until doubled. This will take at least 1 hour, and possibly longer. When it has doubled, bake the loaf in a preheated 350° F oven for 45 to 50 minutes, or until it tests done.

   Note. If you do not use an electric mixer, mix the dough as usual, only allow 2 rising times.

RAISIN BREAD. Decrease the liquid to a total of 1-3/4 cups, and add 1/3 cup white or brown sugar, 2 teaspoons cinnamon, 1 large egg, 1/2 cup raisins and 1/4 cup chopped walnuts or pecans. Bake as directed.

SOY FLOUR BREAD. For maximum protein, decrease the flour used by 1/2 cup and add 1/4 cup each of wheat germ and soy flour. Add these ingredients with the second portion of the flour. Proceed as directed.

WHOLE WHEAT BREAD. If you wish to use whole wheat or graham flour, you must decrease the total amount of flour used by 1/2 cup. Remember also that whole wheat bread should not rise until it is completely doubled, but just about 3/4 of complete proofing. Bake as directed.

Basic Hot Roll Mix

This recipe is also adapted from *Whey Cookery*. It is a simple mix, easy to put together, and very handy to have on the kitchen shelf. The recipe will make a total of approximately 12 dozen rolls, although the mix could also be shaped into loaves and baked. I've only used a few of the variations that are included in the book.

1 cup dried whey powder
9 cups white or unbleached
    white flour
8 tablespoons dried yeast
    granules (8 packets)

1/2 cup sugar
2 tablespoons salt
2 cups skim milk powder
    (non-instant type)
1-3/4 cups hydrogenated
    shortening or margarine

Using a large mixing bowl, combine the whey powder with 3 cups of the flour. Stir together thoroughly to blend well. Then add the remaining flour, the yeast, sugar, salt and milk powder. Stir well. Cut in the shortening as for pie crust. When all is mixed, turn into a 3- or 4-quart storage container, or heavy-duty plastic bag. Store on the shelf or in the refrigerator or freezer.

Basic Quick Rolls

Into a 3-quart mixing bowl measure 2 cups of the Basic Hot Roll Mix. Add 1 cup warm water and stir together quickly and thoroughly. Cover the batter and let it rise for 30 minutes. Then stir in 1 large beaten egg and 2 cups of white or whole wheat flour. Turn out onto a lightly floured bread board and knead lightly, using a little more flour as needed. When the dough is smooth and elastic roll it out and cut or shape as desired. Place on greased cookie sheets, or in a baking pan. Cover and let rise again until doubled. This will take 45 minutes to an hour. Preheat oven and bake at 375° F for 10 to 20 minutes, depending on the size of the rolls. Brush lightly with melted butter when browned and done. Cool on racks, or serve hot.

ONION CHEESE ROLLS. Use the Basic Quick Roll Recipe and add, with the final addition of flour, 2 tablespoons onion soup mix, 1/2 teaspoon dry mustard and 1 cup of shredded Cheddar cheese. Proceed as directed.

Batterway Quick Mix Rolls

Into a 3-quart mixing bowl measure 2 cups of the Basic Hot Roll Mix. Add 2 cups warm water and stir together. Then beat in 1 large egg and 2 cups white or whole wheat flour. Mix well and pour into greased muffin tins, filling them 1/3 full. Cover with a sheet of waxed paper, and let the rolls rise until they are just to the tops of the cups. Preheat oven and bake at 400° F oven for 10 to 12 minutes, or until nicely browned and done. Before you bake these, make certain that the rack is at the upper level of the oven.

Basic Quick Bread Mix

Also adapted from *Whey Cookery,* by Forman and Weeks, this mixture stores well for a just-add-the-liquid convenience. I like to use wheat germ, and in this recipe use 9 cups of flour and 1 cup of wheat germ, as a variation. Remember when using wheat germ or whole wheat flour in mixes that they should be stored in the refrigerator or the freezer.

1/2 cup dried whey powder	1 cup skim milk powder
10 cups white or unbleached	(non-instant type)
white flour (you can use	4 teaspoons salt
part whole wheat flour)	1/4 cup sugar
1/3 cup double-acting baking	1-1/3 cups hydrogenated
powder	shortening or margarine

Using a large mixing bowl, combine the whey powder with 3 cups of the flour. Stir together thoroughly to blend. Then add the remaining flour, baking powder, skim milk powder, salt, and sugar. Cut in the shortening until mixture is like pie crust. Store in a 4-quart plastic storage container or heavy-duty plastic bag.

Quick Mix Dumplings

Combine 2 cups of the Basic Quick Bread Mix with 1/2 cup water and 1 large egg. Stir with a fork until thoroughly mixed. Drop by spoonfuls onto the top of a bubbling hot stew or soup. Cover and cook for 15 minutes without peeking. Uncover and cook 5 minutes longer.

Quick Mix Biscuits

Combine 2 cups of the Basic Quick Bread Mix with enough water to make the mixture hold together without being sticky, about 1/2 cup. Form into a ball and turn out onto a very lightly floured bread board. Pat out to a thickness of 1/2 inch and cut into rounds with a floured cutter. Place on ungreased cookie sheet and brush with beaten egg. Preheat oven and bake at 400° F until browned and done, about 12 minutes.

Quick Mix Muffins

Combine 3 cups of the Basic Quick Bread Mix with 2 tablespoons sugar, 1 large egg and 1 cup milk, water, or thin yogurt. Stir to mix until the dry mixture is just moistened. Spoon into greased muffin tins, filling no more than 3/4 full. Bake in a preheated 375° F oven for 20 to 25 minutes. If desired, sprinkle the muffins with cinnamon-sugar before baking, or add some chopped dates or raisins to the dry mix before adding the liquids.

Quick Mix Pancakes

Combine 3 cups of the Basic Quick Bread Mix with 2 cups milk or water and 2 large eggs. Mix until thoroughly blended and bake as usual for pancakes.

Note. Remember that each time you plan to use any Basic Mix you should shake the container of mix vigorously so that the mix is thoroughly blended before you measure out the amount that you wish to use.

Whole Wheat Whey Bread

Moist and beautifully textured, this bread also slices well, without the crumbling so often associated with whole wheat breads. Please read Success Tips before beginning.

2 cakes yeast	2 teaspoons salt
1/2 cup lukewarm water	1/4 cup vegetable oil
1 teaspoon honey or brown sugar	1/4 cup honey
1/4 teaspoon liquid or granular	1/3 cup powdered whey
lecithin	1/3 cup skim milk powder
2 cups warm water	(non-instant type)
3-1/2 cups whole wheat or	2 cups white or unbleached
graham flour, stirred before	white flour, stirred
measuring	(approximately)

Combine yeast, 1/2 cup lukewarm water and 1 teaspoon honey in a bowl and set aside to proof. In the meantime dissolve the lecithin in 1 cup of the warm water. When the yeast has proofed enough, combine the two mixtures. Add the whole wheat flour and the salt and mix together thoroughly. Then stir in the vegetable oil and the honey. Add the powdered whey and the milk powder to the remaining cup of warm water. Shake together in a blender or in a small hand shaker until smooth. Turn this into the soft dough and begin adding the white flour. Use just enough to make a smooth, medium dough.

Now turn the dough out onto a lightly floured bread board and knead, adding a little more flour as needed, until the dough is smooth and elastic, about 10 to 12 minutes. Then rub the dough all over with a little oil, place it in a clean bowl, cover and let rise until doubled, about 30 minutes. When doubled, punch the dough down and shape into 1 loaf. Place this in a greased 9- by 5- by 3-inch loaf pan. It will fill up the pan about 3/4 full. Cover and let rise about 1/3 more. This will take 15 to 20 minutes in a warm kitchen. Bake in a preheated 350° F oven until browned and done, about 50 to 55 minutes. If it seems a little too moist when you remove it from the oven, just set the loaf, without the bread pan, on the oven rack and bake another 5 minutes or so.

Ninety-Minute Bread

This bread, from start to finish, won't take more than 90 minutes, and may take a little less. If you have one, use an electric mixer with a dough hook. Otherwise you need mighty strong arms, and a slightly longer mixing and kneading time. The whey powder replaces any sugar or milk 100 percent. Be sure to read Success Tips before beginning.

2 cakes yeast	5 cups warm water
1/2 cup lukewarm water	13 to 14 cups whole wheat or
1 teaspoon honey or brown sugar	graham flour (you can
2/3 cup vegetable oil	use half white)
2 tablespoons salt	1-2/3 cups dried whey powder

Combine yeast, 1/2 cup lukewarm water and honey in a small bowl and set aside to proof. In the mixing bowl of your mixer combine the oil, salt, 4 cups of the warm water and 6 cups of the flour. Add the yeast mixture. Combine the remaining cup of warm water and the whey powder and blend, or mix in a hand shaker until smooth. Add this to the flour mixture. Now beat this all together in the mixer, or by hand with a good strong stirring arm, for 5 minutes.

At the end of this mixing time begin adding more flour, using just enough to make a medium dough. If it seems to be too much for the mixer, you can turn the dough out onto a lightly floured bread board and knead it until it is smooth and elastic. This dough does not need a first rising, although if you wish to allow time for it, it will improve the bread. Shape into loaves and place in 3 greased 9- by 5- by 3-inch loaf pans. Cover and let rise for 25 to 30 minutes, or until doubled in size. If you are using all whole wheat or graham flour, then just let the dough rise until it is about 3/4 doubled. Then bake in a preheated 350° F for 35 to 45 minutes, or until done.

Index